First published in Great Britain in 1981 by Virgin Books Ltd.,
61-63 Portobello Road, London W11 3DD.

ISBN 0 907080 15 4

Book design and cover by Martyn Atkins.

Printed in Great Britain by Butler and Tanner Ltd., Frome.
First Edition

Production services by Book Production Consultants, Cambridge

Distributed by Hamlyn Paperbacks, Banda House, Cambridge Grove,
Hammersmith, London, W.6 OLE.

CLUCK!

•

The True Story of Chickens in The Cinema

Jon-Stephen Fink
with additional material by
Mieke van der Linden.

•

Virgin Books

THIS WORK IS
RESPECTFULLY DEDICATED
TO
R. H. W. DILLARD,
PROFESSOR AND PARACLETE

CONTENTS

•

INTRODUCTION
HOW TO USE THIS BOOK
THE EVIDENCE
NOTES
LIST OF TITLES
ACKNOWLEDGEMENTS

1

INTRODUCTION

i. Before the Beginning

Where did chickens come from? This fundamental question has distracted human thinking for hundreds of thousands of years. The perplexing existence of a form of life so palatable and also so ridiculous has formed the foundation of all of the world's meaningful religions. Through the life and death of chickens we have attempted to explain the creation of the world and the significance of human beings.

No physical record of the first coherent thought regarding chickens has survived. We can only imagine the emotions which thinned the sluggish blood of our ancestors at the moment when Cosmic Order was revealed and recognised in a flock of chickens.

It's possible that those primeval emotions gripped the heart and mind of the so-called "Taung baby" (actually a fossil skull) which was discovered by anatomist Raymond Dart in Africa in 1924 and popularized by Dr. Jacob Bronowski on television fifty years later. The Taung baby (*Australopithecus*) may have been the first intelligent creature paralysed by a sudden awareness of the countless stars scattered through the infinite darkness, the certain uncertainty of day changing into night, the difference between male and female, the problems of adolescence, the absolute gulf between what *is* and what *is not* and then to have discovered the peaceful harmony of all things in the vacant clucking of a few plump hens.

"I do not know how the Taung baby began life," Dr. Bronowski wrote, "But to me it still remains the primordial infant from which the whole adventure...began."

ii. A Day in the Life of Australopithecus

In the summer of 1977 scientist-impressionist Eunice van Vliet brought advanced scientific techniques together with artistic intuition to produce a living portrait of the primitive mind. After month-long studies of detailed reproductions of the Alta Mira cave paintings, artefacts excavated from Stone Age burial mounds and fossil skulls not unlike the Taung baby's, Dr. van Vliet sealed herself inside a sensory deprivation chamber. In total darkness and absolute silence, suspended in a pool of water kept precisely at body temperature, her consciousness was catapulted back to its prehistoric origins.

What follows is a transcription of the tape made during this last session in the chamber. Inconsistencies, repetitions and digressions have been edited out for the sake of style.

"My day begins...I stand up to see if it's safe to move...(I hear) a noise...*chut-chut-chut-chtaaaw*...bush chickens (repeated several times)... little pieces of the sun!...(unintelligible) it's not...there's no darkness anywhere I see you...safe, it's safe...Follow them, now, yes! Chickens know where to go...(unintelligible) hole!...Where am I?...Sand...I can't see any chickens anywhere...(or) any water...I need to find a ditch to sleep in..."

If the results of van Vliet's experiments are what she claims them to be, we now have strong evidence to suggest that the search for "meaning" and "order" began tens of thousands of years before civilisation's foundations were laid.

iii. The Red Jungle Fowl or The Red Jungle Fowl

Charles Darwin, during one of his travels to southeast Asia, identified the Red Jungle Fowl as the parent of the modern chicken. This conclusion has never been free of violent controversy.

The question is easy to pose and nearly impossible to resolve: Is the animal that Darwin observed the *Red Jungle* Fowl or the Red *Jungle Fowl*?

For the sake of argument, let's assume that the jungles where this fowl roosted and raised its young were lush with red trees and red bushes. If evolutionary theory is fundamentally sound then chickens, no less than any other creature, carry in their genetic memory the entire history of their life on earth. They would subconsciously "remember" a place very, very different from the modern world — no red jungles exist today.

This theory was put forward in 1931 by Professor Ernst Jodl, who also claimed to have proved the descent of the Jews from a species of salt water trout. An early behaviourist, Jodl suspected that the chicken's easy disorientation, panic and sudden indifference were a result of the harsh contrast between what a chicken's brain *remembers* and what a chicken's eyes *see*.

Ernst Jodl's theory of Chicken Consciousness omits one essential fact — a chicken's behaviour is a function of human perception. What seems to be disorientation or panic to a human observer may be recreation to a chicken. Let's apply this simple logic to the question of the jungle fowl.

Primitive chickens were revered by primitive humans. Chickens appeared to them to be "little pieces of the sun" (see above). This was a crucial connection for our ancestors to make, and one which shaped the course of civilisation as we've come to know it (see below). Consider these points:

1. A red jungle would be much larger than a jungle fowl of *any* colour.
2. If both the jungle and the jungle fowl were red, the jungle would camouflage the fowl, not *vice versa*.
3. A red jungle would appear to be more like the sun than would a ground-dwelling bird.
4. Not a single, isolated reference to trees and bushes behaving like the sun has ever been discovered, deciphered or deduced.

Charles Darwin.

Ancient Chicken.

Dr. Hugo Dexter performed a minor miracle with his address to the American Foundation for the Advancement of Chicken Consciousness in 1976. With one lucid stroke he summarized and defused an explosive argument that has divided societies for generations. He said, "The world just isn't as complicated a place as everybody makes out it is. You can take your politicians and your radicals, and you can take your different life styles and your multi-national corporations and you can divide them into two groups: the ones who believe in red jungles and the ones who believe in jungle fowls."

I owe Dr. Dexter a great debt for those words, and for much else besides. With him I'm committed to the belief that even if red jungles once freakishly occurred in the world, their existence was eclipsed by the spectacular appearance of the jungle fowl. It is from this point that my research and speculation begin.

iv. The King's Bird

Ask any well informed archaeologist and, more often than not, you will hear that the chicken took its place in the human household around 3,000 BC. One archaeologist will say in Burma, another in India (or at least the Indus Valley), still another the Malay Peninsula. But they will *all* tell you that in the fertile land between the Tigris and Euphrates rivers, in the "cradle of civilisation", the cock was known as "the king's bird".

The land and the people of ancient Mesopotamia were rich in chickens and in chicken myths when Sargon the Great became king. One side of a memorial stone believed to commemorate Sargon's coronation bears a portrait of the new king surrounded by his children; on the other side, carved with even greater attention to anatomical detail, is the Sumerian symbol for Nature — a lean rooster raping a fat hen.

Nature is depicted as the balance between male and female, a basic formula which begins with chickens and leads to the gods. To Sargon,

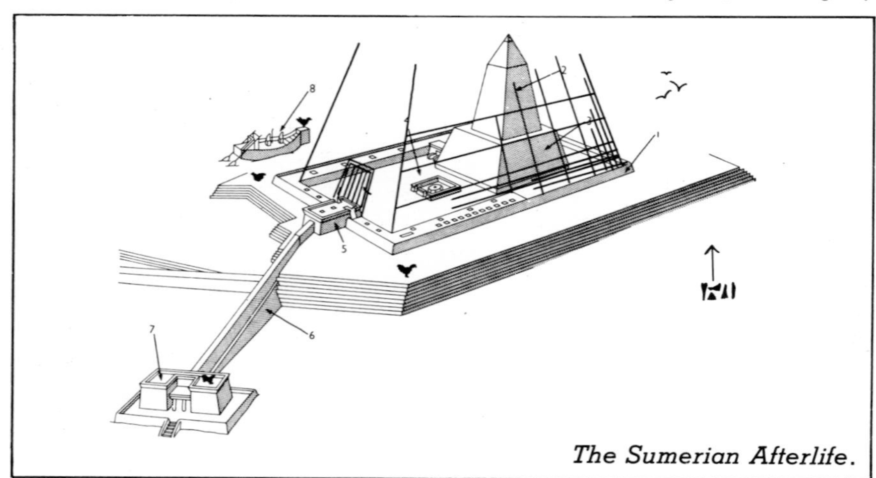

The Sumerian Afterlife.

the universe was defined by the passions of gods and goddesses, whose activities were visible on earth in the daily lives of chickens. This concept was a refinement of the primitive idea, "Chickens know where to go" (see above), and it was nothing less than the high noon of real religion. If the lives of the gods (meaning the movement of the universe) were there to be seen in the never changing relationship of roosters and hens, the purpose of human life must be to reflect the same order and achieve the same deathless perfection. To Sargon, the world was divided between male and female, rooster and hen, up and down, himself and everybody else.

The idea of the world and the universe from the point of view of "everybody else" in the Sumero-Akkadian Empire fits neatly into the picture that Sargon drew. Humans, they were convinced, were made of clay mixed with the blood of a slaughtered god and were created for one purpose only: to be the servants of chickens by supplying them with food and shelter so that they might rest from the heavy obligation of spiritual life. Fatalistic and resigned, they were sure that humans had no free will, that they were helpless and had only to accept meekly and submissively the fate dealt them from the "chickenworld" (*Hühnerwelt* in Geismann's translation). There is a line from a fragment of Sumerian wisdom text which perfectly captures the common world view: "Never was a chickenless child born to his mother."

Both king and commoner looked forward to life after death. Peasants believed that the afterlife would appear to them as a great, poorly maintained chicken coop where royalty, high officials and those who had taken the best care of the greatest number of chickens occupied the most desirable perches. Royalty, on the other hand, told each other that when they died their souls flew into the beak of a crowing rooster, where their sound and strength could continue to influence lives on earth.

The Sumerians had over 200 words to describe the moods of chickens.

v. The Riddle of the Pyramids, *Solved*!

For one brief period in Egyptian history, Egyptian peasants were happy. The root cause of this happiness was the rise to the throne of Akhenaton in 1380 BC. While not in itself an occasion for unrestrained joy — ordinary Egyptians continued to lead lives of monotonous drudgery, raising water chickens for trade and taxes — it was the first time that peasants were told by their king that their own pathetic lives and deaths meant something. Having little reason to do anything else, they believed him.

Akhenaton's revolutionary idea was that the sun, Aton, should be worshipped as the only god. More momentous than this leap of faith, however, was Akhenaton's mystical revelation that the chicken was Aton's second favourite earthly creation.* These ideas, branded "heresy" after Akhenaton's death, are celebrated together in the intricately beautiful "Hymn to the Aton"!

Praise to Aton...
Who makes the chick speak within its shell.

Outwardly, the commoners' lives were completely unchanged; inwardly, they glowed with an uncommon happiness. After Akhenaton's "revelations" the dreary work of draining the coops, floating the feathers, puncturing the beaks and the rest of the endless water chicken routine became both a spiritual test and a spiritual lesson. A lesson in this life, to teach human beings how to behave and a test which would decide the soul's fate.

After death, every soul entered the Hall of Judgment where it was met by the god Anubis, who had the body of a man and the head of a chicken. Anubis weighed the soul on a scale, balancing it against a chicken heart. If the scales balanced it proved that in life the soul had learned its lessons and had become chicken-like in body, mind and spirit. If Anubis was satisfied, he allowed the soul (the *ka*) to go on to the "good place" or the

* The favourite was Akhenaton.

"happy place". But if the scales failed to balance, the *ka* was roasted on a spit, eaten by Anubis then excreted onto a pile of chicken droppings.

When Akhenaton died, the Egyptian empire was ravaged by war, disease, insurrection, boredom, frustration and madness. As in any modern state these conditions made it possible for power to be seized by heartless military despots. Faced with the problems of controlling the people and rebuilding the empire, one solution presented itself to the ruling elite: order slaves to build pyramids.

This solution was not without problems of its own. There was a practical problem: how to feed the teeming mass of slaves. There was a morale problem, too. The pharaohs who came after Akhenaton destroyed every trace of his influence — the temples he built were torn down, every scroll which bore his name was burned, the docile water chickens and those who tended them were remorselessly butchered. Deprived of their livelihood, of the very meaning of their lives, forced to move tons of sand and rock from one end of the desert to the other or until they were starved to death or dropped from exhaustion and exposure, most Egyptians were unhappy. Mass suicides were common and there was a real danger that the pyramids would never be completed.

The Nineteenth Dynasty resolved this new crisis with subtle genius. They built incubators – incubators capable of hatching up to 10,000 chicks at a time. The incubators provided food for the labouring masses *and* a vivid illustration of the new meaning of life and death. Here were thousands of chickens with only one reason to exist: to appease the desires of the pharoah.

Even though none of this made the Egyptian peasants *happy*, they were content that life made sense again. The pyramids were built. Against all odds they have survived fundamentally unchanged for millennia, but they survive not as monuments to the power of the pharaohs of the New Kingdom — they stand as mute witnesses to the decline and fall of an entire civilisation. The essential meaning of the chicken was subverted by brutes to a crude demonstration of brute strength. The soul of the people, hopeless and retarded, perished.

vi. The Greeks were Curious, the Romans were Depraved

Athens in the 4th Century B C was famous for the natural curiosity and imagination of its philosophers. Fearless and confusing men, they were tenacious in their pursuit of truth, beauty and young boys. A seminal and penetrating thinker, Socrates was forced to poison himself after the Council of Athens found him guilty of "impiety" and "corrupting the youth" — the cruel fact is that he was put to death for loitering around cockfights.

The accusation and conviction were unusually unfair in the light of the fact that cockfights in ancient Athens were as easy to avoid as Athenians. The cock was celebrated as a potent symbol of virility — an expression of masculine beauty and of the masculine principle even more profoundly expressed as philosophical courage. For these reasons, cockfights attracted adolescent boys and consequently, philosophers.

Naïve boys ("students") gathered at the feet of older men ("philosophers") to absorb wisdom that would prepare them for mature life. This wisdom took the form of *lines of argument*. Wandering through the audience of an Athenian cockfight 2,400 years ago, we would have heard these *lines* rise clearly above the cheers and jeers of the ordinary spectators.

A Sophist might use a cockfight to prove that rule by force is a law of nature, while a Hedonist would use it to prove that seeking pleasure is Nature's fundamental urge, therefore good, and a Cynic meanwhile would teach that it demonstrates the futility of struggling against Fate.

Of all the voices vying for attention, one would be the clearest of all, one man's voice the surest and most persuasive, the ageless voice of

The Acropolis, Greece.

Socrates. Cockfights stirred the Greek soul to action, inspiring the mildest of men to perform acts of selfless bravery and heedless risk. Socrates probed the reaches of innocence and experience to attach some sort of meaning to events caused by men imitating roosters. The "students" (young boys), attracted to him by his *line*, became men whose influence would be felt for thousands of years in every part of the world. One of these boys was known to Socrates as Plato.

After hearing Socrates' spirited argument with Laches on the subject of courage —

SOCRATES: Would you say that courage is a nice thing?
LACHES: Very nice.
SOCRATES: And cowardice is evil and hurtful?
LACHES: Yes.
SOCRATES: Do you want to see what I'm hiding under my tunic...?

— Plato abandoned himself to the old man and his strenuous effort to discover the Ideal on earth. The two lived as master and apprentice in a cave on the outskirts of Athens where they promoted cockfights, seduced stray and idle men and argued the finer points of courage (see above), piety, duty, liability and the immortality of the soul.

On his deathbed, Socrates reminded his old friend Crito, "We owe a cock to Aesculapius," an ironic reference to the ritual of thanksgiving for the recovery of sexual potency. The remark was typical of Socrates' talent for condensing the sum of human wisdom and fallibility into a few simple words.

Plato was 30 years old when Socrates died. After a long absence, the student returned to Athens as its greatest teacher, establishing the Academus (Academy) and ending his life embittered, rejecting the senses as a source of truth. Western thought is based on his idea of reality.

Polyarchus, a wealthy and respected Roman citizen, was one of the few residents, and possibly the last, of that city to have understood the importance of chickenkind to humankind. When one of his adored roosters or hens died, he gave it a public funeral and erected a monument to its honour. When Polyarchus died, his neighbours merely felt relieved of a harmless if annoying "eccentric". If they had a fraction of Polyarchus' sensitivity, they would have seen in his death the beginning of the horrific end of the Roman Empire.

As they did with the arts and the law, Romans looked to classical Greece to find a model for a *modus vivendi* between humans and chickens. Characteristically, the Roman *modus* perverted flesh and feather alike and to a degree of depravity unrivalled until the present century. The cock became identified with Eros, the god of erotic love and through Mercury with wealth, the acquisition of money and gambling.

The debasement of the chicken was transformed into a fine art at the court of Caligula. Seeking light entertainment and distraction from insomnia, he would often summon slave girls for the *danse du poulet*.* The girls squatted on small alabaster platforms at one end of Caligula's bedroom. At the other end, at Caligula's command, six chickens were released from a silver filigree cage. The girls attempted to attract the birds by whatever means occurred to them — clucking softly, offering food, impersonating a rooster or by pretending to be paralysed with fear. The body of the girl who attracted the fewest chickens was smeared with chicken fat and thrown into the palace kennels. The howling went on for days. The 19th Century poet and dramatist P.H. Hulme captured the horror of Caligula's reign in his blank verse epic, *Errata:*

> Many were the dark nights and long
> When heard I him pacing
> From marble floor to marble floor,
> Amidst the shrieking of wenches
> And the shrill cackling of uneaten hens...

* Bonmarcher's translation.

Costumes for an early Goldwyn epic. No executive at MGM was prepared to "go on the record" to reveal anything about the movie in which these chickens were used.

Nero, not to be outdone, took fiendish pleasure in dressing chickens in little togas and replacing members of his court and government with them. While the respect he paid to chickens was inadvertently fitting and proper, both human spirit and chicken spirit were vulgarised for the sake of a trivial joke.

Chicken abuse was not limited to the ruling class. Holiday entertainment for the Roman public always included spectacular displays of cruelty to animals. During festivals, crowds of 50,000 would gather at the Colosseum and 260,000 at the Circus Maximus to ogle gladiatorial combat. Brutal spectacles were staged by the government to occupy the time and attention of idle Romans who would otherwise run riot. By the time of the twilight of the empire more than half of the days of the year were holidays commemorated with such "spectaculars".

Suetonius, Tacitus and Juvenal all record the blood sports which were played even by children. The most popular one, outside of the organised "games" at the Colosseum and Circus Maximus, was "chicken baiting". A chicken was tied by one foot to a sturdy pole. A few kernels of corn were dropped on the ground in front of it and when the bird began to peck at them the "baiter" stepped forward and crushed its head with a mallet. Thousands of chickens were dispatched in this way every day.

But it was in the great circuses where the Roman soul, that bizarre mixture of grandeur and perversity, emerged. The "Tournament of Beasts" was the epitome of chicken madness, often celebrated with 5,000 animal casualties in a single day. Impresarios strained their imaginations to organise unequal contests — a rooster against a lion or panther, a hen against twenty men armed with bows and arrows. The chickens were stupefied with fear, the uncomprehending crowd merely stupefied, the profound connection between them irredeemably broken.

In the later years of the Roman Empire, chickens' lives were reduced to non-sequiturs, attracting only ridicule and derision. Following the same path that Egypt took centuries before, Rome strolled blindly into the abyss. The "eternal" city was sacked twice by Asiatic barbarians, "primitives" — who knew the true value of a chicken.

vii. Paradise Regained, Or...?

Which are the events that future historians will call the milestones of the 20th Century? The First World War, the "war to end war" reshaped the map of Europe and made a second world war inevitable; the Great Depression spread like a cancer throughout the industrialised world, tainting every level of society; World War Two redistributed the balance of power and made the Cold War inevitable; the Atomic Age, the Space Age forced back the spiritual and physical frontiers for the first time in thousands of years. At each of these historic crossroads, America was there.

In the throb of the American heartbeat was nothing less than the hope of Western Civilisation. America — rough and tumble doughboys, hand in hand with Tommy in the trenches, beating back the Hun; America —

 Wall Street, the epicentre of global economic collapse; America — dogface G.I.'s on Pacific beachheads and in European villages, spitting in the face of Fascism; America — blazing the way into outer space, setting a human being down on the surface of the moon...

Underneath the war and peace, underneath the ebb and flow of world economies, underneath the changing fortunes of people and places the fate of Western Civilisation was in the hands of unpredictable, unheroic men and women — American film-makers. Working "behind the scenes" of history, directors, actors, writers, set designers and producers struggled to re-establish the link with the chickenworld.

In secrecy, scripts were written, sets were designed, scenes were directed and productions orchestrated in such a way to reveal the presence of chickens. The task of reuniting human beings, their most profound fears and boldest aspirations, with the spiritual harmony of chickens fell to the Hollywood dream merchants, the artists who composed the pictures that the masses carried around in their heads.

The film industry (as it was destined to become) was understandably shy about turning chicken consciousness into any kind of crusade. One man thrust the idea before the public before its time and paid dearly for his effort. When Jack Nelson directed *Chickens* for Paramount Studios in 1921 he expected to usher in a new age of popular awareness. What the release of his film met with was speechless horror effectively disguised as general indifference. Nelson never again worked with such righteous passion.

Others in the industry experienced the harsh example of Nelson's martyrdom. The "chicken network" retreated underground, evolving over the years into a secret society. Its existence is consistently and adamantly denied by functionaries and luminaries alike, but evidence of its influence began to emerge in 1975.

In January of that year, college-aged men and women in movie audiences in Virginia* stood up and shouted "Cluck!" whenever a chicken appeared on the screen. By summer, movie houses across the country were visited by so-called "chicken patrols" who loitered in the lobby loudly denouncing a film for failing to include chickens "in a single line of dialogue or a single foot of film." As disturbances like these multiplied, a clear message was broadcast to Hollywood: the stage is set for revelation.

Probably during the decades of practised secrecy, film makers stifled the desire and lost the capacity to trust other people with the truth. Yet in the scant six years since the first tremors were felt in Virginia, several prominent (not to say eminent) directors, writers and producers have come forward from the shadows to shout "Cluck!" Many have put their careers at risk to reveal one of the least known and least discussed secrets in the bitter-sweet history of civilisation.

During the course of our research, we were intrigued by persistent rumours about an organisation known only as "the Council". Its

* Specifically in the Roanoke Valley.

An "open call" screen test in 1942.

membership, it was hinted, is drawn from the higher echelons of the film industry. This "Council" allegedly decides when, where and what kind of chicken scene will be in a film. These decisions apparently are made at semi-annual meetings held in Petaluma, California[1]. One director suggested to us that financing for a film is made available — or unavailable — by decision of this "Council". If we were to consider the implications of this sort of "evidence", we would be led to the conclusion that *for the sake of chickenkind* the business of movie-making has become a refuge for corporate megalomaniacs whose sole reason for existence is to exercise power over genius!

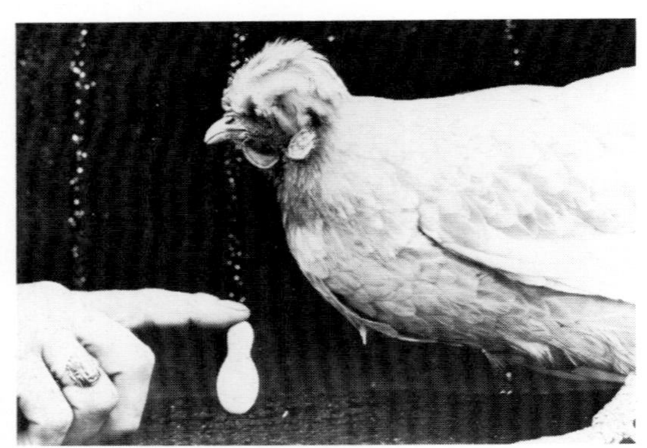

Special effects hands prepare a matte shot for 'Village of the Giants.'

13 It bears mentioning at this point that this book was researched, written and published in the face of desperate odds and relentless opposition. Our hope in light of that fact is that the words and pictures on the pages which follow will serve as a signpost to mark the way we have come and the place we are today. The shape our future will take depends upon the measure of our courage. We must not shrink from recognising that our redemption — from pain, from tyranny, from disaffection, from meaninglessness and chaos — resides in universal awareness of the interwoven fates of chickenkind and humankind. That awareness in modern times is enshrined in motion pictures, the ultimate refuge of ultimate truth.

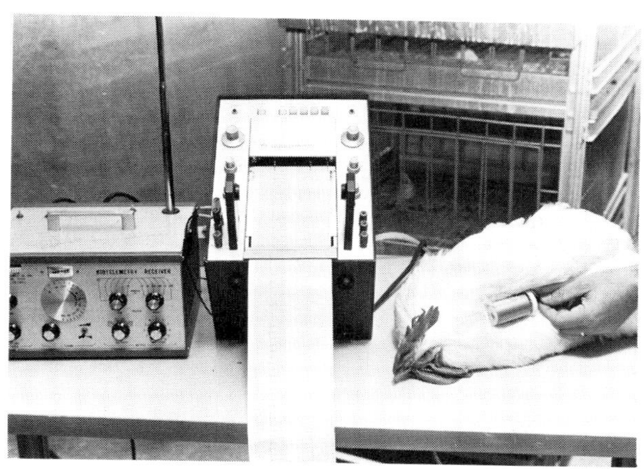

The "perfect chicken" is measured and tested at a meeting of the Council in Petaluma, California. We believe this picture to be authentic.

HOW TO USE THIS BOOK

1. *How chicken scenes are defined.* Before the significance and consequence of a film can be judged, its chicken scene must be identified. Films without chicken scenes deserve to be dismissed as trivial distractions comparable to dance contests or beauty pageants. *Use this book as a manual to distinguish the varieties of chicken scenes,* **verbal** and **visual**.

Visual chicken scenes include the presence of:

- living chickens (a flock or an individual cock or hen)
- dead chickens (plucked and butchered or otherwise)
- uncooked chickens (whole or in pieces)
- cooked chickens (baked, boiled, broiled, fried, etc., served whole or in pieces)
- chickens artistically rendered as figurines, statues, weathervanes, paintings, photographs, wallpaper designs, etc.
- the words "chicken", "hen" or "rooster" graphically displayed, as on a sign.

Verbal chicken scenes include the occurence of:

- the words "chicken", "hen" or "rooster" in a line of dialogue, narration or incidental music
- derivative expressions such as "chickenshit" or "henpecked"
- names such as Rooster Cogburn, Little Red Henski, etc.

Note: The presence of eggs does not in itself determine a chicken scene. The egg or eggs must be accompanied by a direct or indirect reference to chickens*. The same applies to the presence of feathers.

2 . *How these chicken scenes are rated.* The value of a chicken scene (and consequently the value of the film in which it occurs) is measured according to its involvement as an element of theme or plot. A chicken in a primitive ritual, for instance (as in *Apocalypse Now*) does not carry as much thematic weight as a chicken in a bedroom (as in *Ma and Pa Kettle at Home*). *Use this book as a guide to assess the value of chicken scenes.*

3 . *How these chicken scenes are arranged.* The scenes are arranged alphabetically by the title of the film in which they appear. Principals (directors, writers, producers, etc.) are included in the same array and are cross-indexed with the film titles. *Use this book as a reference and keep a copy close at hand.*

4 . *How chicken consciousness will be raised.* The audience in a movie theatre is really no more than a sampling of the total population collected in a big, dark room. When you go to see a movie and when a chicken appears on the screen, react instinctively: shout, "Cluck!" so that the moment receives the attention it deserves. *Use this book as a manifesto.* Carry it with you and keep it visible. If you are asked questions about chicken consciousness, answer clearly and politely. The quality of life in our time and in the years to come depends upon the circulation that this book and these ideas enjoy. Our fate is in your hands.

* For an example of eggs appearing with a direct reference to chickens, see *Catch-22* and for an indirect reference, see *In the Realm of the Senses*.

THE EVIDENCE

17 *A BRIDGE TOO FAR* (1977)

Director Richard Attenborough and screenwriter William Goldman wove the themes of this sprawling World War II epic into a chicken scene of poignance and prophetic wisdom. Packed inside a Dakota aircraft are the paratroops about to hurl themselves feet first into irredeemable disaster. We see the faces of the soldiers on whom the Grim Reaper has had a claim since the opening credits. The last of these courageous and expendable young men carries a knapsack. Out of the knapsack pokes the head of a chicken, zestfully alive, playfully curious and like his human companions, doomed to die.

The vignette underscores Attenborough's central theme of absurd particulars combining into absurdity of historic proportions. The essential reference is to the chicken's woeful inability to achieve true flight. The hen is taken into the sky in an airplane — an airplane and the sky are two places where chickens manifestly do not belong. Ironically, human beings (like chickens) are unable to fly to great heights unaided by some device. The sting of that irony is intentional.

Later in the film the paratrooper, who earlier carried the knapsack, appears instead with a flame thrower; there is no sign of the chicken. The chicken's dramatic disappearance is meant to imply the futility of life during poorly planned military operations.

See: Barron, Steve; *Catch-22*.

Where is the chicken?

The Fab Four in 'A Hard Day's Night.'

A HARD DAY'S NIGHT (1964)

In the early Sixties it was the Beatles who felt the urge to plant the seed of chicken consciousness in the fertile midst of the mass of "young adults". Soliciting the advice and directorial skill of Richard Lester, John Lennon and Paul McCartney sought to depict the distance that had grown between their generation and chickens the world over. The problem of how to reconcile the devil-may-care irreverence of the "lads" with the gravity of their message was left to the formidable talents of writer Alun Owen. After weeks of brainstorming, the solution was found.

A scene was written for George Harrison, known as "the quiet Beatle". His apparent seriousness and sensitivity formed a perfect bridge between the medium and the message. Idle yet inquisitive, George wanders into an office at the television studio where the Beatles will perform. An assistant whispers into her desk phone, "We've got one of them!"

On his way into a marketing executive's inner sanctum, Harrison plucks the harp-like tail of a metal sculpture. It is a sculpture of a rooster. "You don't see many of these anymore," he muses, and seems to mourn.

United Artists believed it to be in the best interest of the film to leave the scene uncut, though revised. The first draft was rumoured to have included on the soundtrack an unreleased Beatles cover version of "Chickenfoot":

If ya cain't chicken foot, ya cain't dance nothin'.
Ya chickenfoot, neck and gizzard,
My black gal is slick as a buzzard.[2]

The front office allegedly suppressed this version as "subversive", a characteristic which would undercut the Beatles' image as "the acceptable face of modern counterculture"[3].

See: *Rock 'N' Roll High School*.

ALL THAT JAZZ (1979)

Bob Fosse's masterful crypto-autobiographical ballad of an artist/entertainer's life on the edge is riddled with intimations of mortality. Roy Scheider is Joe Gideon, a compulsive choreographer whose physical and emotional life suffers for the sake of "showtime". Crisis comes in the shape of a heart attack, which sends the irrepressible Broadway kingpin into hospital. From his bed he lamely recites to a visitor the week's menu. On Tuesday the entrée is chicken.

In his hospital gown, reclining, helpless and weak, wrapped in the white sheets of his adjustable bed, stretched out under the fluorescent light, Gideon's pallor foreshadows the boiled drumstick he will certainly be served, if he lives until Tuesday.

Page Smith observes, "Just as it is necessary to break a perfect egg to make an imperfect omelette, it is necessary to kill a chicken to prepare it for the table." Just as the chicken dinner moves closer to him with each passing second, so he moves toward Death.

Fosse asks us to regard boiled chicken and death alike as irresistibly female. Playing on the inevitability of the one entering our bodies and our bodies entering the other, this scene poetically reduces every choice we make in life to one unambiguous question: Will our appetite now be satisfied by boiled chicken?

See: *Annie Hall*.

ALL THE PRESIDENT'S MEN (1976)

Ordinary Americans commemorated America's bicentennial in ordinary ways — with barbecues, firework displays, costume parties and prayer meetings. Extraordinary Americans blessed with influence in show business and ownership of a "hot property" used the occasion to make forceful, relevant chicken statements. Robert Redford drew such a statement from the shadows of political intrigue.

Redford, as Washington Post reporter Bob Woodward, meets his informer "Deep Throat" (Hal Holbrook) deep in the bowels of a subterranean garage. For months now Deep Throat has guided Woodward on a fateful path, advising him to "follow the money", a clue which has led the journalist to the brink of an amazing discovery. At a crucial point in the investigation Deep Throat retreats further into the

shadows, his information is vague and unhelpful, he seems to be stalling or holding out. Woodward's patience is at an end: "Listen, I'm tired of your chickenshit!"

The chicken is invoked as an image of order (government). By extending that symbolism specifically to the Nixon administration, Woodward characterises its by-product as excreta ("-shit"). The contrasting by-product is, of course, eggs, which as food nourish life and when fertilised engender it. Chickenshit can boast neither quality. There is no doubt about where Redford & Company stand on the Watergate question.

After this film was released chicken sales soared, especially during the July 4 week-end. That pinnacle of awareness has since suffered a measurable decline.

See: *Being There*.

ALICE DOESN'T LIVE HERE ANYMORE (1972)

After her brutish husband is killed in a road accident, housewife Alice Hyatt (Ellen Burstyn) is suddenly free to make a new life. She leaves New Mexico and travels West, looking for work as a resident singer in a small bar. Chicken presence is felt all through the film, intricate references which illuminate the obscure complexities of a life in transition.

With a deceptively friendly overture, a man leads Alice to a booth in a lounge in which the bar owner is sitting. The lines are worth repeating verbatim.

LENNY
Uh...Chicken, I'd like
you to meet Alice...um...
Alice...

ALICE
Alice, Alice Hyatt.

CHICKEN
Mighty nice meeting you, Miss...

ALICE
(overanxious)
Hyatt.

CHICKEN
Chicken Holliman. Would you
be kind enough to turn around
for me?

While the *polli ruspanti* (free ranging hens) enjoy the benefits of an uninhibited life style, they live exposed to abiding danger. Alice's odyssey, that of the modern woman, from lame acceptance to dynamic self-expression can be described in the words quoted by the Reverend Edmund Saul Dixon, "Liberty and *varied* abundance are the two greatest essentials for poultry, old and young, to promote health, growth, beauty and fertility."[4]. Alice's liberty though is more a perilous burden than a health and beauty aid. The spectre of sexual possession stalks her like a hairy beast.

Working steadily as a waitress in Mel & Ruby's Café, Alice overhears the salty banter between the owner, Mel (Vic Tayback) and another waitress (Diane Ladd).

MEL
Why all the talk about sex? Am
I getting you all bothered up?

FLORENCE
I could lay under you, eat fried
chicken and do a crossword puzzle
all at the same time, that's how
much you bother me.

Alice reels inwardly, yet her expression does not betray the memory of the indignity she suffered at the hands of Chicken Holliman (Dean Casper). Her thoughts are turning toward the hope and fear of romance with David (Kris Kristofferson).

In the original draft by Robert Getchell, Florence's line, "I could lay under you, eat fried chicken..." was intended to foreshadow a pivotal scene between Alice and David. Inexplicably, the lines were rewritten.

While mending a fence on his farm David opines, "The only thing stupider than a cow is a chicken. I'd like to kill every leghorn on this place." In the final draft the chickens were dropped and a turkey anecdote used instead.

Speculation is wide-ranging about the reasons for the rewrite. The most reasonable suggestion, made to us "off the record" by people who were there is that director Martin Scorsese refused to film a scene that was in any way derogatory to chickens. The film he made preserves an essential understanding of the chicken as a touchstone in unsettling times.

See: Burstyn, Ellen;

ANIMAL HOUSE (1978)

> I gave my love a cherry that had no stone,
> I gave my love a chicken that had no bone...
>
> —The Riddle Song
> (American Traditional)

The moral contest between American society and the American anti-social *avant-garde* began to gather momentum in the autumn of 1962. The overt convulsions of that struggle are dramatised on the fictional campus of Faber College. During a "frat" party, a suave undergraduate bachelor serenades a demure coed. He strums his guitar softly and sings the first verse of a gentle folk song (see above). The couple gaze dreamily into each other's eyes.

Gazing unsympathetically on that witheringly sentimental couple is Bluto (John Belushi), the personification of irreversible social malaise. Bluto's reaction (more a reflex) is swift and effective — he smashes the guitar against the wall.

In conversation with us, John Landis, who directed the production for Universal, explained that this minimal nod to chickendom was in fact the pivotal scene. An egg, he pointed out (i.e., the solution to the song's chicken riddle) is a metaphor for the social unrest that would "hatch out" in the mid- and late-Sixties. That possibility aside, this chicken scene disappointed the hope Landis raised a year earlier when he directed *Kentucky Fried Movie*.

See: Landis, John.

ANDERSON, BOB

See: Pepe 1 and Pepe 2.

23 *ANNIE HALL* (1977)

Woody Allen's Academy Award-winning portrait of a "nervous romance" marked his emergence as an accomplished film-maker with a subtle apprehension of modern life. The polarity he explores through the twists and turns of a love affair between comedian Alvy Singer (Allen) and naïf Annie Hall (Diane Keaton) finds expression in two gem-like chicken scenes.

Allen returns with authority to come to terms with his favourite enigma, that of a man's compulsive need for love and sex and the levelling inevitability of death. Well into the story, when it is clear that their affair is all but over, Alvy and Annie struggle through a weekend together in Los Angeles. Alvy lies nauseous on his hotel bed, attended by a doctor. As he catalogues the symptoms of his misery he unconsciously, compulsively, nibbles shreds of chicken from a plate. The chicken is mere meat, pale and dead. Eating it he internalises the death of his romance with Annie. In the plane on their way back to New York, wordlessly and then with words unvarnished by sentiment, they admit the inescapable truth: the affair is over.

As an artist Allen is far too shrewd to "carry" all of his "eggs" in one "basket." With the final lines of the final scene, he and co-author Marshall Brickman offer us entry into the film's deeper meaning. Reflecting on his now past romance with Annie and on romances in general, Alvy recalls an appropriate joke. Our research has turned up the earliest documented version of that joke, which varies only slightly from the Allen-Brickman text.*

ZIP: Say, Pip. You know that my brother thinks that he is a chicken!

PIP: Why, that is very strange, Zip. Will you take him to a "head doctor"?

ZIP: I would, don't you know, but we need the eggs![5]

His lover may be lost to him, but not his need to love; chickens may be neglected by us, but not our perpetual need to know them. In other words, as long as chickens are remote from our lives we are bereft of any reasonable hope. Seen in this light, the earlier chicken episode becomes a quiet sermon on the connection between our acceptance of chickens and our acceptance of dying. We need to digest (as Alvy digests the shreds of chicken) the little deaths that are the ends of love affairs, of friendships, of vacations, of events which culminate in the ultimate death: death.

*Told by Alvy, the lines are updated. *Will you take him to a "head doctor"?* becomes, *Why don't you take him to a psychiatrist?* The punchline remains essentially unchanged.

See: *All That Jazz; Blue Angel, The; Catch-22.*

APOCALYPSE NOW (1979)

Tremedous public interest surrounded Francis Ford Coppola's uncertainty over which of two endings his film would have. Reputedly, on the strength of the reactions of preview audiences to the two versions, the question resolved itself.

In both versions, the murder of Colonel Kurtz (Marlon Brando) by Captain Willard (Martin Sheen) is intercut with footage of a Montagnard (Philippino) ritual slaughtering of a bull. In one version, however, a tribesman is seen moving through the crowd carrying a large white chicken on his shoulder. Soon after, the chicken (or its twin) is in the hands of a tribeswoman; she shakes the bird violently up and down. In a second version, neither the tribesman, the tribeswoman, nor the the chicken is seen. In the end, Coppola chose to include the exotic chicken footage.

The point he makes is clear, although the reason — commercial or artistic — for his uncertainty is not. The comparison of the two rituals, Kurtz's murder and the slaughter of the bull, would be meaningless if the chicken were absent: where would the connection be? With the chicken present though, Coppola makes a serious point: no matter how advanced our technology (the motorboat that brought Willard up river to Kurtz), our motives and our lives are primitive — our choices are decided by the conditions of physical existence.

Because of monsoons and the high cost of petroleum products, this film was very expensive and took a very long time to make.

See: *Emmanuelle*.

ARGOS CAFÉ

Situated across the street from the old Samuel Goldwyn Studios, the Argos has been looked to as a stirring reminder of the fundamental reason for motion pictures to exist. Its heraldic rooster crowing atop a sturdy steel pillar can be seen for blocks. At its tables some of the most significant "deals" were hammered out and in its shadow many of the most memorable chicken scenes were conceived, developed and shot.

When *Gone With the Wind* was in pre-production, Uncle Peter's chicken scene was cut by Victor Fleming, who feared that its aggressiveness would undercut the pathos of Scarlett O'Hara's starvation. Producer David O. Selznick meditated on the problem during a walk along Santa Monica Boulevard, a walk which brought him past the Argos. He saw the Argos rooster and then demanded unequivocally that the "last chicken in Atlanta" scene remain untouched.

Limousines are often seen parked in front of this café.

See: *Gone With the Wind.*

Argos Café, Hollywood.

BABE RUTH STORY, THE (1949)

His fans all called him the Sultan of Swat and he called them all "keed"; his parents called him George Herman but the face that smiles out from the bronze plaque in the Baseball Hall of Fame is the one every American knows simply as "Babe". He was the greatest ball player of his day and, when his story came to be told on film, his biographers took special care to portray him as a man whose consciousness embraced chickens.

Ruth's career was seldom free of controversy. There was no one in his life with whom he clashed more dramatically than he did with Yankees manager Miller Huggins. The incident, which writer Bob Considine and director Roy Del Ruth considered pivotal in the Babe's life and story, concerned a wounded dog, a frightened little boy, a celebrated surgeon and a famous truancy.

During a practice before a game, Ruth (William Bendix) hits a searing line drive which a sprightly puppy fields with its ribcage. Heartsick over the pain he has caused, Ruth takes the dog and the little boy who owns it to a large hospital. He uses his influence to engage the service of a skilled surgeon, who saves the dog's life. Meanwhile, hours have passed and Ruth has forgotten that he is supposed to be playing in a baseball game.

Of course, he arrives too late and must face the wrath of Miller Huggins (Dick Lane). Huggins suspends Ruth for the rest of the season and fines him $5,000. Furious about such a judgment Ruth curses the scrawny Huggins, calling him a "little chicken neck".

What Ruth is suggesting is this. A chicken neck is far from meaty, just as Huggins is. This is a "macho" taunt and one to be expected from an athlete. Chicken esophogi (windpipes), ground or chopped, were believed to be a cure for bedwetting. Not only his stature now but Huggins' virility is insulted.

Were Ruth (despite his name) and Huggins (despite his) homosexual lovers? Considine offers us no real clues. Cockfighting is indirectly evoked — the scene is set in the locker room, a place where men undress together. The taunt itself is a *goad*, figuratively resembling the spurs made of steel or bronze which are attached to the legs of duelling bantams. Nevertheless it is a skirmish which Huggins had already won.

The tragic poet Ion wrote, after witnessing a cockfight, "He falls to earth not yet crushed in body or both eyes by the blows, but with failing strength he groans and refuses to be a slave"[6]. At least as much had to be said for the Babe.

Crowds flocked to the opening of 'The Babe Ruth Story' when word of its emotionally wrenching chicken scene reached the streets. 'Raw Deal', a film without a chicken "in a single line of dialogue or a single frame of film", closed shortly after this picture was taken.

27 *BAD COMPANY* (1972)

Frontier morality — what do those words really mean? Robert Benton attempted a definition with a story about a marauding gang of juvenile outlaws who are led to petty triumphs and absolute tragedy by a charismatic sociopath.

Kid criminal Jake Rumsey (Jeff Bridges) puts together a rag tag band of orphans and castaways who will learn to wring at least a living from the new settlers of the Old West. Rumsey is at first joined then opposed by the benign Drew Dixon (Barry Brown). In the early days of this uneasy alliance, hunger and chickens, chickens and morality and reward and punishment together become a single volatile issue.

Physical survival comes at the cost of spiritual extinction. To survive they must eat and to eat they must steal chickens. This powerful chicken larceny scene unfolds in a barnyard. Symbolic of society, the barnyard attracts, one might even say provokes, the young desperados. The flock of chickens there is large, healthy, beckoning. The fledgling outlaws throw themselves into a free-for-all that is unparalleled as a picture of humanity's spiritual hunger. In the end it is only Rumsey who emerges with a chicken.

When the living (objective) chicken is transformed into roast (subjective) chicken, Dixon asks for his share. Rumsey refuses to give him any, bluntly pointing to the fact that Dixon didn't help to steal it. Critics fell short of classing this film with religious dramas set in Biblical times, but it must now be regarded as a "testament" of chicken gospel. The living chickens as objects of human desire and the roast chicken as an object of human appetite are the source of the faltering power of the devil-god.

See: *Badlands; Blues Brothers, The; Bonnie and Clyde; It Happened One Night; Rocky II; Sin Town.*

A violent moment in 'Bad Company'.

BADLANDS (1974)

In 1958 Charles Starkweather, 19, and his 14-year old girlfriend Caril Fugate took off on a murder spree through the Midwest which resulted in the deaths of ten people. Terry Malick's fictionalised rendering of their story recalls the generally "primitive" and specifically Sumerian belief that the universe is itself malicious and must be appeased.

Kit Carruthers (Martin Sheen) sweeps impressionable, pubescent Holly (Sissy Spacek) off her feet, out of her house and into a whirlpool of crime and chaos. Their existence is not without a certain romance — their hideout is a treehouse. Nor are their lives expressions of mindless evil — they keep chickens close to them in handcrafted cages.

Malick weds the concept of sacrifice with the indomitable spirit of American individualism. Kit is a deviant, yes, a murderer, yes, but he carries in his psychotic character the dark side of America as it was in the 1950s — raw energy straining for spiritual form . The chickens are Kit's and Holly's access to the "godly", just as homicide delivers them into the "ungodly". When they are visited by Kit's friend Cato (Ramon Bieri) Kit offers him a legbound chicken saying, "Here. You take that sombitch." It is a gesture both of surrender (a sacrifice to the gods) and a retreat into the darkness of mayhem.

It would be wrong to see Terry Malick as a pessimistic artist. The image of this "sacrificial hen" recurs in the film he made five years later, *Days of Heaven*. Again, he is particularly concerned with the life and death of the chicken as the fulcrum which balances redemption and damnation.

See: *Bad Company* ; Malick, Terence.

Steve Barron

29 *BARRON, STEVE*

For three years Barron, who was the clapper-loader on *A Bridge Too Far*, has maintained an impenetrable silence about that film's chicken scene. His unwillingness to tell what he knows to be the facts surrounding, for instance, the fate of the chicken, has not gone unacknowledged. He now describes himself to American immigration authorities as "a man of independent means" whose life style is currently supported by "dividends" from recent "investments". Barron spends up to 20 hours a day in his swimming pool in Encino, California. He gave no direct answer to any of our questions, asking us instead to watch him so that "the tide" didn't carry him "into the ocean and over the edge of the world." His house has no telephone.

See: *A Bridge Too Far*.

BEING THERE (1979)

Two chicken incidents mark the transformation of a simple-minded gardener called Chance (Peter Sellers) from cloistered misfit to celebrated political pundit. Chance embodies the very innocence of Eden and his life forms a bridge between the vegetable and human worlds. Hovering (figuratively) at his elbow are, inevitably, chickens.

Chance's entire apprehension of reality derives from television, it is a constant feature of his life. As he watches a children's show one morning he is told by the housekeeper that, "The old man is dead." On television, a sad harmony. Buffy St. Marie sings about love. Chance idly switches to another channel and we hear yet another children's show host say, "There are plenty of animals in the barnyard. Wanna go with the rooster and see 'em?" A rooster puppet lopes across the screen and the host crows, "Cock-a-doodle-doo! Cock-a-doodle-doo! Cock-a-doodle-doo!" It is Chance's Great Awakening.

Forced out of the house and home that had been his sanctuary since he was a child, Chance wanders out into the "barnyard" of the world outside. Just as had been promised, there are "plenty of animals" there. On a Washington, D.C. sidestreet Chance meets a young black hooligan (Oteil Burbridge) who immediately confuses him with someone else. "Did that chickenshit asshole Raphael send you, boy?" he demands to know.

Chicken manure is a basic ingredient of compost. Rich in nitrates, it makes a potent fertiliser. As a gardener, Chance understands that. The "hip" idiom in no way confuses him, he instinctively apprehends the meaning: his opinion about a fertiliser ("chickenshit") called "Raphael" is being solicited ("Did that...send you?"). His keen insight which some might carelessly dismiss as mental retardation, saves him from becoming another violent crime statistic.

Hal Ashby, a director who can be counted on for consistent if conservative chicken scenes (*Harold and Maud, The Last Detail*), depended on screenwriter Jerzy Kosinski to create unimposing chicken incidents. While these may be fairly regarded as rather subtle, it is clear from the undeveloped potential inherent in the work that Ashby chooses to remain "in the coop" until someone tells him that it is safe to come out.

See: *All the President's Men*.

BENTON, ROBERT

As a writer and director, Benton is directly responsible for two of the more thoughtful chicken scenes of the 1970's. He declined to meet with us — why?

A possible explanation may lie in further speculation about the presence of the so-called "Council". After having decided that the Best Picture Oscar would be won by *Kramer vs. Kramer*, they decide that it is now in their best interest to keep Mr. Benton busy. His letter adopts a cordial, impersonal tone, as if it were written by committee or a computer. While "Benton" does nothing to confirm or deny deliberate use of the chicken in his work, he *does* consider our invitation for him to unburden himself "kind interest ".

Our offer for him to meet us somewhere halfway mysteriously went missing. Consequently our reservation at the Motel 6 in Denton, Kansas had to be cancelled and our deposit forfeited.

STAB PRODUCTIONS
110 West 57th Street
New York, N.Y. 10019

July 31, 1980

Mr. Jon-Stephen Fink
Mr. Mieke van der Linden
473 South Bedford Drive
Beverly Hills, CA 90210

Dear Mssrs. Fink and van der Linden:

Thank you for your letter of May 26th. Your project certainly sounds like an interesting one, however, I'm afraid I am not going to be able to be of much help to you. I am currently in pre-production for my next film which begins shooting in late October and with my hectic schedule it looks like I'm not going to have any time to meet or confer with you.

I do thank you, however, for your kind interest, and I wish you the best of luck with your project.

Sincerely,

Robert Benton

31 *BLUE ANGEL, THE* (1930)

Josef von Sternberg has written of his involvement with this first German sound film, "In conveying the substance of Mann's story to me (Emil) Jannings was superb, his eyes sparkled, and I began to analyse the ingredients that were to form the basis for *The Blue Angel.*"[7]

The story of the decline and fall of Professor Immanuel Rath (Jannings) at the icy hands of chanteuse Lola-Lola (Marlene Dietrich) has become legend. Rath and Lola are all men and all women, fatally attracted to each other by psycho-sexual forces beyond their control.

At their marriage their friend Kiepert (Kurt Garron), a sleight-of-hand artist, makes an egg appear from under Rath's nose. "Now, I'll produce another egg," Kiepert says and a second egg appears. He hands Rath the egg and sits down.

> LOLA looks sideways at RATH and begins to cluck like a hen.
> RATH sits holding the two eggs. At first he looks surprised, then grinning happily, he suddenly crows like a cock.

The marriage of Rath and Lola is an allusion to William Blake's "Marriage of Heaven and Hell". Rath's proud crowing will become a pitiful mockery of manhood when, penniless, he must act as Kiepert's onstage patsy.

Kiepert repeats his "magic egg" trick for a full house in a *boite* in Rath's home town. "An ordinary hen's egg," Kiepert announces before he breaks it on the professor's head. Finally, he offers Rath a simple proposition: "If you don't crow now, I'll kill you". The audience shouts, "Lay another one! Lay another one!" as Rath refuses to crow for his tormentor.

Offstage, Lola enjoys a young man's passionate embrace. Rath staggers toward her and "crows hoarsely at the top of his voice like a madman."[8] Pursuing Lola to her dressing room Rath stands in the doorway, puffs out his chest and lunges at her. As he strangles the life out of her, her screams mingle with Rath's shrill, mournful crowing.

This was Emil Jannings' finest hour and his only featured chicken scene. His uninhibited performance as a man of learning who perverts his life and that of the chickenworld in the sleazy demi-monde deeply affected producer David O. Selznick. When Alfred Hitchcock met with Selznick to discuss casting for *Rebecca*, the producer was quick to nominate Jannings. "But," Hitchcock pointed out, "Jannings is dead." Selznick spoke from the heart: "He'll do it for me."[9]

See: *Annie Hall*

A wedding gift from Kiepert (Kurt Gerron) to Professor Rath (Emil Jannings) causes Lola-Lola (Marlene Dietrich) to cluck contentedly. A scene of foreboding in von Sternberg's 'The Blue Angel.' ▶

LOLA
LOLA

33 *BLUES BROTHERS, THE* (1980)

Reaffirming the hope raised in 1977 when he directed *Kentucky Fried Movie*, director John Landis has placed himself in the vanguard of

John Landis (left) sets up the "fried chicken scene" in 'The Blues Brothers.' With him are, from left, John Belushi, Dan Aykroyd and Aretha Franklin.

progressive artist intent on raising chicken consciousness. His "musical comedy", which shares the qualities of prophetic vision and *delirium tremens*, moves the chicken from the shadows into the limelight.

John Belushi is Jake Blues, just out of prison after doing his stretch for armed robbery. In order to raise enough money to pay the county assessment on the orphanage where he and brother Elwood (Dan Aykroyd) were raised, the defunct Blues Brothers Band has to be revived. Their "mission" takes them to the café where "Blue Lou" Marini and Matt "Guitar" Murphy work, respectively, as chief cook and dish washer.

Jake and Elwood sit at the counter and place their orders. Elwood orders "one piece of dry white toast ". Jake asks the owner (Aretha Franklin) whether she has any fried chicken. "Best fried chicken in the state," she boasts. Jake orders four fried chickens and a coke. The production number Franklin performs here is "Think".

The stage in the club where the band performs its first "gig" is enclosed by chickenwire . This in itself would be of only passing interest, the banal image of a stage which is also a cage. What distinguishes this scene is the line spoken by guitarist Steve Cropper: "Chickenwire?"

Indeed. When the rowdy clientele responds to the Brothers' rendition of the theme from "Rawhide" by hurling beer bottles at them, as a sympathetic audience we are relieved that chicken wire protects the musicians so effectively. Landis plays on an interpretation of chicken-wire very different from the more traditional concept of chickenwire as "a means or tool of confinement"[10] favoured by film-makers such as Franco Brusati (*Bread and Chocolate*).

Associated here as they are with modern urban "outlaws", the chickens exist only on the fringes of popular awareness. Only here, it seems, beyond the pale, is the presence of the chicken keenly felt. The "mission from God" (as Elwood refers to their escapade) is to inspire awareness and sensitivity in the population at large. Life will be no easier for the prophets of chicken consciousness than it was for the prophets of Judeo-Christianity.

Physical damage is inevitable in the process of enlightening the benighted. In this case, a shopping mall and more vehicles than can be counted fall in the Blues Brothers' wake. Neatly insinuated is a counterpoint to the *motif* in Robert Benton's *Bad Company* — spiritual survival may be at the cost of physical extinction.

See: *Bad Company; Bonnie and Clyde; Bread and Chocolate* ; Landis, John.

BONNIE AND CLYDE (1967)

Fried chicken speaks to us from the days of the Depression in Arthur Penn's glamorisation of the lives and deaths of Bonnie Parker and Clyde Barrow. The Barrow gang, notorious and fun-loving bank robbers, have eluded local, state and federal law officers all across the Midwest . After settling into a cosy bungalow to recuperate from the terrible pressures of life on the run, the gang agrees that some kind of dinner needs to be rustled up. Buck Barrow (Gene Hackman) remembers passing, "a chicken place down the road". Bonnie (Faye Dunnaway) and C.W. Moss (Michael J. Pollard) offer to go out again to pick up the food.

When C.W. pays for the order of fried chicken, with Bonnie standing at his side, another customer notices the revolver that the outlaw carries in his waistband. The police are alerted. As a result of the ensuing ambush, Buck is killed, his wife Blanche (Estelle Parsons) is blinded, Bonnie and Clyde are critically wounded.

Fried chicken is a ghostly guide to the death of the lawless. Just as Virgil led Dante through damnation to salvation, so fried chicken leads the forces for good (law and order) to battle with the sinful until sin is eradicated. As Nature abhors a vacuum so chickens abhor chaos. An icy drumstick points to the Barrows from the other world.

The moralistic theme of this film is one of the few pieces of evidence which can be cited to substantiate rumours that "invisible hands" were at work formulating the chicken scene. Significantly, Penn was "unavailable" to meet with us and tacitly allows this aspect of his film to be regarded, in the words of his apologists, as "personal inspiration".

See: *Bad Company; Blues Brothers, The; Faster, Pussycat! Kill! Kill!.*

BORN TO KILL (1979)

See: *Cockfighter.*

BREAD AND CHOCOLATE (1978)

Franco Brusati's poignant essay on *la condition humaine* casts Nino Manfredi in the role of a hapless Italian immigrant worker swimming against the tide of the Swiss mainstream. He is the personification of the undesirable alien in us all.

At his lowest ebb, having lost his job, his room and his work papers, Manfredi is lured to a farm operated by Italians who share his plight. He is greeted by an old, old man.

The open yard where the two men stand is alive with milk-white chickens. The old man leads Manfredi into a building and tells him that the place is a slaughterhouse. We follow along outside as they walk through, the old man detailing the steps which transform living chickens into cold freight. The tour ends at a set of wooden racks where a hundred chicken carcasses hang drying in the sun. Manfredi and his guide emerge covered with white feathers and the old man casually observes, gesturing toward the carcasses, "They look just like humans." It is clear now that Brusati's subject is humanity's evolutionary fate.

From the abattoir Manfredi is invited to the house where the old man and his family live. Their house and home is a rudely converted chicken coop. Tiny bedrooms are separated from one another by thin curtains, each the place where a married couple sleeps, except the last cubicle, which belongs to a nephew. Does he sleep alone? The curtain parts and we see a fat white hen nesting on the bed. The physical union of humans and chickens is made reverently explicit.

The rest of the family now files in to eat lunch, which is of course, chicken. A little boy, his hair improbably combed straight up to mimick a rooster's comb, cheered on by his relatives, crows his innocent heart out. Soon the lunch has become a bacchanal of chicken imitations — the men flapping their boney arms in ritual praise of chickens, cackling, clucking, demented and enraptured.

They are distracted from their frenzy by the arrival in the woods beyond of the sons and daughters of the farm's Swiss owner. Fine-boned, fair-skinned, blonde heirs and heiresses cavort in the nude in the woods, and in the mountain stream. Manfredi and the rest, still covered with white feathers, watch them from behind a fence of chickenwire, from

beyond an unbridgeable gulf.
an unbridgeable gulf.

Brusati's vision is of ultimate chicken consciousness, when human lives will blend totally with chicken lives. It is a hopeful vision of the future, a prophecy that promises a time when the world will be divided between humans who have taken the inevitable evolutionary step — bodies and minds that are in equal part human and chicken — and those who have not. The silent, shattering tableau is a vision of the moment when *la condition humaine* becomes *la condition poulet.*

See: *Blues Brothers, The; Freaks.*

'Bread and Chocolate' — chickens before... and after.

37 *BRIDE OF FRANKENSTEIN, THE* (1935)

In my beginning is my end...
— T.S. Eliot
from *Four Quartets*

One of the fundamental laws of Nature is that human beings tamper with the Natural Order at their peril. We remember electric toothbrushes, Sensurround and edible underwear. Yet each generation "seeking good, doing evil" has to learn the lesson all over again. When James Whale directed *The Bride of Frankenstein*, neither electric toothbrushes, sensurround nor edible underwear were milestones in human history. Whale needed to look elsewhere for an example of human folly.

Not having learned the lesson taught by the life and times of the first Frankenstein monster, Doctor Pretorius (Ernest Thesiger) blackmails Doctor Frankenstein (Colin Clive) into manufacturing a mate for the lonely prototype (Boris Karloff). Pretorius dictates his plan, "We will make a *woo-man.*"

When we first meet Pretorius, sinewy, weasel-like, "cultivated", he sits eating supper in a crypt, a tomb for his table. The tomb contains the remains of a recently deceased young girl, the source of most of the components that will go into fabricating the bride. The recent remains of the doctor's meal rest on top of the tomb: the partial skeleton of a chicken.

The chicken bones, meatless, featherless, useless, lie inert on the cold stone. Death and doom hover in the air around Pretorius. Whale was one of the few directors to insist that chicken presence is only the manifestation in "our world" of an active cosmic intelligence. His radical view is shared only by "occultists", but in general terms his description of the chicken principle is consistent with the conventional concept. Whale would describe the crypt-chicken as an omen of the "vengeance" this cosmic intelligence will visit on aberrations of nature — Pretorius and the two Frankenstein monsters. Conventional chicken theory would describe the acts and consequences as the restoration of "natural balance". The crypt-chicken *signifyies* this process.

In the climactic scene set in Frankenstein's laboratory tower, the Monster speaks with a new voice, "We belong dead!" The tower explodes and collapses—the fatal "revenge" promised by the skeletal chicken. Whale never explained why, if cosmic intelligence corrects perversion and aberration, the world continues to deteriorate.

BROOKS, MEL

Emerging now as the motivating force behind substantial dramatic films, Mr. Brooks believes that people now want to return to a romantic yet unsentimental vision of the chicken.

The History of the World, Part I is an attempt to elevate chickens to

Inspired after a chicken dinner, Dr. Pretorius (Ernest Thesiger) presents the bridegroom (Boris Karloff) to the father of the bride.

Mel Brooks.

 genuine political consequence. Since the fearsomely dynamic Brooks has taken this bold, deliberate course he has become isolated. His lonely crusade has aroused suspicion and uncertainty down the corridors of power in the Hollywood establishment. As a defensive manoeuvre, high security surrounds his office at Twentieth Century Fox, lending it the atmosphere of a throne room. Clearly, he is unsure about the nature of the repercussions resulting from the radical direction of his new work.

The time we spent with him was memorably enhanced by his spirited renditions of a wide range of light classics including "The Chicken I Love" and Irving Berlin's "The Chicken Doodle-doo".

See: *History of the World, Part I, The.*

BUGSY MALONE (1977)

Alan Parker has composed a modern parable which describes contemporary American business practice as the reincarnation of the religious life of Nero's Rome. Just as chickens were used as fetishes surrounding material gain in the temples and salons of Rome in the First Century AD, that symbolism and the behaviour it inspires, Parker tells us, is a compelling feature in Twentieth Century American society.

Fat Sam (John Cassissi) is a gangland overlord locked in the throes of a power struggle ("gang war") with a lean, hungry and ruthless racketeer. A goodhearted loner, Bugsy Malone (Scott Baio), falls in with Sam so that he can acquire the means to bankroll his girlfriend's singing career. Throughout the violent, convulsive episodes the cast, all of them children, personify America as a "juvenile" whose actions are motivated solely by self-gratification[11]. During an intense car chase, Fat Sam's sedan crashes through a barn. He emerges unhurt and with a chicken on his lap.

If we take Parker's implication at face value, free enterprise (the car chase) recklessly creates openings for little more than ritualised theft (the chicken). On a slightly deeper level though, Fat Sam is the expression of the American dream gone wrong. Chickens don't just "fall into" one's lap, although a chicken *does* fall into Sam's. Where thousands of American workers stood in soup and bread lines in years past and today overcrowd "rescue missions", businessmen who pursue the fruits of other people's labour and acquire them through extortion, robbery, wage-slavery, murder and worse, may come to possess chickens. Even if such a person rewards loyalty or succumbs to sentiment, his real function is as an emblem, a warning of what we can become by regarding chickens as dispensable "commodities".

See: Introduction, *vi.*; *Catch-22;* Parker, Alan.

Fat Sam (John Cassissi) reveres his latest acquisition in Alan Parker's 'Bugsy Malone'.

E L L E N   B U R S T Y N

July 28, 1980

Dear Mr. Fink and Ms. van der Linden,

I am currently involved in a play in New York, so will not be travelling to Los Angeles in the foreseeable future, and am therefore unable to discuss your book with you.

With best wishes,

Sincerely,

Ellen Burstyn

Ellen Burstyn

Ellen Burstyn — whom is she protecting?

BURSTYN, ELLEN

Under the direction of Martin Scorsese this actress, as Alice Hyatt, shares a tense scene with a character named Chicken Holliman in the film that established her as a bankable film performer. We believe that the letter we received from her was indeed written by Ms. Burstyn, but its terse finality suggests that its composition benefitted from the "advice" of someone else. "With best wishes" is a closing favoured by writers of promotional and bulk mailings.

She tells us that she is "unable to discuss" the subject of this book with us. Based on the evidence of her letter, we believe that she is telling the truth. Several unacknowledged telegrams and unreturned phone calls convinced us that too much is at risk for Ellen Burstyn to talk. Whom is she protecting?

See: *Alice Doesn't Live Here Anymore*;Malick, Terence.

BUTTONS (1927)

Director-writer George Hill, echoing the popular desire to find some reason to go on living during the hopeless years of the Lost Generation, made a film celebrating the virtue of American youth. Uncompromising moral standards and an uncomplicated perception of reality combine in the character of Buttons (Jackie Coogan) to stand as a bulwark against wilful perversion of chicken charisma.

Buttons becomes a cabin boy on the transatlantic liner *S.S. Queenland*. The ship is commanded by Captain Travers (Lars Hanson) who is accompanied by his beautiful fiancée, Ruth (Gertrude Stratton). Ruth is pursued by the roué, Henri Rizard (Roy D'Arcy), who resorts to disguising himself as a chicken to secure valuable time alone with her. Ever faithful to Captain Travers, Buttons fights a steady rearguard action which preserves Ruth's honor, the Captain's dignity and his own place as a valued and trusted crew member. Despite all of this the *S.S. Queenland* sinks and the word "erection" is not permitted to be used in theatrically released films for another 40 years.

Wardrobe was by Gilbert Clark.

'Buttons'(Jackie Coogan)makes life difficult for shipboard Romeo Henri Rizard (Roy D'Arcy)

CATHCART
What is it, Lt. Minderbinder?

MILO
An egg, sir.

CATHCART
I know that, Lieutenant.

MILO
A fresh egg, sir.

CATHCART
Where did you —

MILO
In Malta, sir — where there are enough chickens
to lay fresh eggs for every officer
in the squadron at 5c
a piece from the mess fund.

CATHCART
Yes?

MILO
With a clear profit of 2c per egg.

CATHCART
For whom?

MILO
Sir — for whomever sells the eggs to the mess.

Is awareness of chickens a moral value relative to a particular time, place and circumstance, or is that awareness, along with all it entails, an absolute and constant value? One answer to that fundamental question is proposed in Buck Henry's elegant adaptation of Joseph Heller's novel. The short answer is that there are acts and there are consequences — human beings are essentially victims of genetically unstable entrepreneurs.

The scene between such an entrepreneur, Milo Minderbinder (Jon Voight) and his superior, Colonel Cathcart (Martin Balsam) is a vivid illustration of the intricate morality of war. On the one hand, Milo promotes chicken consciousness among American Army officers through greater distribution of chicken eggs. On the other hand, Milo's profiteering (of which the eggs and Maltese chickens are the initial

Milo (Jon Voight) displays an egg.

manoeuver) results in Allied fatalities (Art Garfunkel). Betrayal and death stem directly from what has to be seen as the exploitation of chickens.

That exploitation though, began with devotion. The conflict raging around Milo is a mirror image of the conflict raging in his soul. War has perverted the capitalist ideal, the American expression of chicken consciousness. In peace-time, Milo would own and operate a profitable mail order house in Petaluma, California, sending incubators and fertile eggs everywhere in the continental United States, but war has twisted his ambition and distorted his vision. He uses chickens as a stepping stone to physical and moral autonomy — a frightening travesty of the natural order.

During war, everyone and everything loses its innocence.

See: *A Bridge Too Far*; *Annie Hall; Bugsy Malone; Egg and I, The;* Henry, Buck.

CHICKENS (1921) 🐔🐔🐔🐔

Jack Nelson directed this historic motion picture, the first modern chicken statement to reach the silver screen. This "comedy-drama" chronicles the move of society "swell" Deem Stanwood (Douglas McLean) from the big city to the peaceful countryside. Settled on his farm, he decides to raise chickens.

Stanwood's investments, left in the hands of trustees, are mismanaged, his fortune is lost, his farm fails and he is forced to mortgage it to Willie Frig (Raymond Cannon). Not only the fates of his chickens are in jeopardy. Frig is his rival for the hand of the lovely Julia (Gladys George). Julia, tormented by the plight of Stanwood's chickens, takes over the mortgage and marries him.

By choosing a woman to be both the avenging and guardian angel, Nelson portrays chickens in their feminine aspect — receptive, merciful, fertile. The farm comes to signify *shelter* — physical shelter from the elements and spiritual shelter from the chaos of modern urban life. On that level, the chicken coop performs the same function for the chickens. The nests themselves are comforting signs of perpetuation, of hope for many tomorrows. Into this Eden comes Deem Stanwood.

Failure, first of his fortune then of his farm, point to the frailty and fallibility of human life in general and of rich, spoiled men in particular. Chickens and those close to chickens can be moved to teach people the true meaning of "love" and the way to achieve salvation (freedom from mortgages).

Nelson was concerned that there was too little chicken presence in the world, which had just endured a devastating war. Sensing that no improvement was forthcoming from the literary, artistic, musical or industrial quarters, he took the burden upon himself. To a large extent the character Julia embodies Nelson's attitude toward both chickens and human beings. The moments of his film, shot by shot, become fixed in one's memory like stars in the night sky — a close-up of Julia near the chicken coop, Deem's joy when his mortgage worries are over. And like stars, these moments, taken together, are like the constellations. Both real and abstract, they reflect and influence the fates of humans individually and of humanity as a whole.

Chickens was an ambitious film, perhaps too ambitious for its time. While Nelson never returned to the theme himself, his work did influence and encourage other young directors. Henry Leherman directed *Chicken à la King* for Fox in 1928, Victor Herman directed *The Chicken in the Case* for Selznick in 1921, and *The Chicken that Came Home to Roost* was the working title that King Baggot had to suppress in favour of *Town Scandal*, made for Universal in 1923*.

See: Introduction, vii; *Egg and I, The*.

* It's ironic that the site of Universal Pictures was at that time called Taylor Ranch, owned by UP boss Carl Laemle. The income from the ranch derived mainly from its large flock of chickens.

45 *CHICKEN BOY*

Towering an imposing 40 feet above Broadway near 5th Street in downtown Los Angeles, this statue marks the geographical centre of chicken consciousness. Film-makers and film executives spend their lunch hours here in the restaurant at the statue's base or suspended from ropes strung from adjacent office windows to Chicken Boy's beak. The beak is stroked as a gesture to solemnise the consummation of a "deal".

The original of the Chicken Boy statue (destroyed in the 1926 earthquake) was carried back from Egypt by D.W. Griffith who intended to use it to adorn the set of *Intolerance*. It is a representation of the god Anubis (see Introduction, v.), which once guarded the tomb of Ramses II. Afraid that the statue would be desecrated, or worse, by disaffected marketing and middle-management people, a slush fund, (maintained as the "savings account" of John Doe in a bank in Petaluma, California) supported a 24-hour security service. After the earthquake a fried chicken restaurant was installed in a room forming the plinth. Most people believe that the Chicken Boy statue standing today is the 3,000 year old original.

See: Weitzman, Lew.

Chicken Boy.

CHICKEN EVERY SUNDAY (1949) 46

Dismissed by mainstream critics as "stodgy", "a potboiler" and "simple-minded", this film remains one of the true mysteries of Hollywood's cultural history. It has not seen theatrical release for three decades. Heralded by the gossip columnists as "the ultimate chicken statement" and an example of "responsible popular art destined to open the floodgates", the picture's release date curiously coincided with the initial investigations of Senator Joseph "Tailgunner Joe" McCarthy and the House Un-American Activities Committee. The blacklist which resulted put thousands of artists and technicians out of work.

The basic values which are celebrated by Jim Hefferen (Dan Dailey) and his wife Rosemary (Celeste Holm) were interpreted as obvious "red herrings", diverting suspicion from the film's Marxist message. Millie Moon (Connie Gilchrist) is the ex-Vaudeville lush and Geoffrey Lawson (Alan Young) is the asthmatic bachelor fatally attracted to her — their "apache dance"[12] according to the senators, represents the seduction class being seduced by the "fat cats" of capitalism. The HUAC investigators did make one valid point, and that is that the ambiguous "sausage scene" confuses the question of the relationship between humans and chickens.

After the "witch hunt" ended, *Chicken Every Sunday* was considered by studio executives to be "out of touch" with the popular taste and its re-release date was pushed further and further back.

Jim Hefferen (Dan Daily) lends a subtle irony to Sunday dinner in 'Chicken Every Sunday'.

47 *CHINATOWN* (1974)

Jack Nicholson is J.J. Gittes, a private investigator who inadvertently untangles a web of corruption spun by a powerful real-estate pirate, Noah Cross (John Huston). Roman Polanski, whose treatment of chickens always tends toward the metaphysical, worked Robert Townes' screenplay around a chicken scene which defines moral obligation in a climate of sexual and political manipulation.

Gittes is invited to Cross's estate for lunch. The meal is fish and it is served whole, its dead eye staring up at the detective. Cross apologises, "I hope you don't mind. I believe they should be served with the head." Gittes takes a second to frame an answer. "As long as you don't serve chicken that way."

On the immediate level, on which Gittes functions, "serve" has only one meaning -prepare.But on a broader plane, the area Cross surveys, that word has a double meaning –not only prepare, but *to be used by*[13]. While the reference could be faulted for being arcane, the Sumerian concept of the human/chicken relationship is far from irrelevant. Gittes' quip then, "As long as you don't serve chicken that way," is a message to Cross from the chickenworld — "Be active in our service, not passive, like a dead fish."

See: Introduction, iv; Nicholson, Jack.

Detective J.J. Gittes (Jack Nicholson) accepts an invitation to dine with powerful Noah Cross (John Huston). Gittes is lucky that chicken wasn't on the menu!

Hundreds of thousands of words have been written on the subject of Orson Welles' genius and of the finest flower of that genius, *Citizen Kane*. Yet the words on this page are the first which reveal the hidden meaning of the chicken scene which at one time had the power to redirect the of the American cinema.

Welles' unique vision allowed him to look deeply into the minute structure of the world and there see its history, its condition and its destiny. This quality, of course, made him attractive to the members of the newly formed Council who were responsible for determining policy. An invitation was extended to Welles for him to become President *pro tem* during the transition of Hollywood's chicken interests from informal lobby to chartered congress. Welles declined. As a result of his personal experience with the fledgling Council he had momentous things to say about the art and politics of the motion picture business, and by extension, American culture and society. Soon after his first and only meeting with Council emissaries, Welles undertook production of *Citizen Kane*.

The period in the life of Charles Foster Kane, which perfectly paralleled the complexities and contradictions of the chicken issue in Welles' life, was the tycoon's courtship of cabaret songstress, Susan Alexander. One incident in that courtship (one scene in the film) epitomises the romance of "the prince" and "the showgirl".

Kane (Welles) and Susan (Dorothy Comingore) are alone in her backstage dressing-room. They are at ease with each other, playful and uninhibited, more like schoolmates than lovers. Kane shows off his skill at wiggling his ears and Susan giggles encouragingly. His act goes on. He entertains her with a shadow puppet. With the light behind him, he holds his hands in such a way that the shadow they cast is magically altered. "What is it?" Susan begs, "Is it a giraffe?" Kane is delighted by her girlish innocence. "No, it's supposed to be a rooster." And so it is. Kane's knuckles form the comb, his thumbs the beak. The figure floats on the wall, larger than life, and then is gone.

"Rosebud" was the last word that Charles Foster Kane spoke on earth. We now know that *Rosebud* was the name of the bobsled Kane had when he was a boy. Why did Welles include this "trivia" in his film biography of a great and powerful man? In part, "Rosebud" is an insight into Kane's character. He was his entire life a man-child, the two aspects of his personality alternately emerging. But Rosebud was more than an emblem of Kane's ever-present childhood: Rosebud was a red herring.

In light of the "solution" to the "mystery" of Rosebud, the shadow rooster is a childish distraction for Kane from the toil of maintaining "the sixth largest personal fortune in the world". It is a dalliance in the same way that his romance with Susan is a dalliance. But Welles' true intention was to warn those who would be most affected, that a new beast was slouching toward Bethlehem. Through Kane, Welles speaks as a film-maker whose responsibility and pleasure it is to entertain an audience —

Kane entertains Susan with an image projected on a wall just as Welles entertains us with the image projected on the screen. But his "magic lantern" show has much greater dimension than that. The rooster's image is both tangible and intangible — visible, but insubstantial except as an idea.

Specifically, the shadow rooster is the sinister spectre of the Council. It arises in the lives of a romantic couple, which Welles employs as a metaphor for two film partnerships: producer and director, and director and audience. Clearly, he saw a power there which could be used for the good of all or abused and hoarded by an unresponsive elite. He raised an alarm which people would not or could not hear.

Orson Welles managed to make only a handful of films after *Citizen Kane*. Now, an artist idolised by film-makers the world over, he remains on the fringes of the industry. Hounded into obesity by radical elements of the Council, he appears now only in advertisements for wine and mineral water and in cameo roles in the feature films of much less talented directors.

CLOSE ENCOUNTERS OF THE THIRD KIND (1978)

Will other life forms comprehend fried chicken? Steven Spielberg is one of only two directors of "speculative" (science fiction) films to regard the chicken as a focal point of the story and its meaning.* After the central United States is visited by a squadron of Unidentified Flying Objects, Roy Neary (Richard Dreyfus) and other interested Hoosiers gather to watch and wait for a second visitation. Families, couples, senior citizens sit on car roofs, blankets and at tables. On one table lies an unopened box of Kentucky Fried Chicken.

As Neary enters the alien spaceship at the film's end, the homey, earthly image of the box of fried chicken returns to us. The chicken is being taken light years away from Earth "inside" him. While Spielberg never makes explicit the fact that Neary had *eaten* the fried chicken, or indeed that any was even offered to him, he implies that such a leap of faith must be made. This "giant leap" for humanity lands us firmly on the other side of the "final frontier". If human consequence is to be carried to the stars and beyond, it must be on the wings of chickens. Not even Jacob Bronowski felt competent to speculate about the way chicken would be perceived by, for instance, silicone-based life forms endowed with special effects far in advance of our own. Spielberg wisely leaves such speculation to our scientists; his concerns are purely existential.

See: International Chicken Flying Meet, The.

* The other is John Carpenter.

'Cockfighter'.

COCKFIGHTER (1979)

As it ever was, so shall it remain. The cock has been prized as a living symbol of virility for millennia. The relationship of man to man (and through that the relationship of man to woman) is rendered in its starkest aspect here by screenwriter Charles Willieford and director Monte Hellman. The story is one long tableau showing us the essential stuff of which humans are made.

Frank Mansfield (Warren Oates) is a celebrity on the cockfighting circuit who vows to win the Cockfighter of the Year medal. As we follow the ebb and flow of his fight to the top, we see a mythical yet personal link forged between the fate of the cockfighter (Everyman) and that of his fighting cocks.

That relationship, by the time shooting was completed, was keenly felt by all of the cast and crew. A cockfight was being filmed which Mansfield's bird was supposed to win. The cock challenging his was to be a "runner" — a bird who "turns tail" (chickens out), and so ends the fight. The technical adviser found a bird known to be a runner. Mansfield's bird had won fight after fight. Three cameras were set up in the pit and rolled for 10 minutes with the "runner" showing no signs of quitting. As soon as the cameras were reloaded and the fight resumed it was Mansfield's bird that sprinted out of the pit. The "coward" crowed his victory and the dialogue between Mansfield and his opponent had to be rewritten on the spot to match the action of the chickens. How many times must the same lesson be taught?

The fight between two cocks in a ring is a primal battle for sexual dominance. Each cock is an extension of each cockfighter's masculinity. Cocks are much more than the animate symbols of virility, they are as they fight, its measure. Hellman was quick to apprehend this aspect of cockfighting and stressed a love interest between Frank and a woman to comment on the curiously low incidence of homosexuality among American cockfighters.

See: Hellman, Monte; *What's Up, Tiger Lily?*

The Marx Brothers, Harpo (left), Groucho (centre) and Chico (right) brought the chicken into motion pictures by submerging it in a popular vaudeville "bit".

COCONUTS (1932)

The Marx Brothers can always be relied upon to illuminate the deepest reaches of the human character by way of absurd exaggeration. Their work has been compared to the work of Ionesco, Duchamp and the Russian Futurists — and not without reason.

In *Coconuts*, Groucho is an unscrupulous hotelier and real estate salesman named Hammer . Hammer hires Chico to be his "shill" at a local real estate auction. Hammer has to give his accomplice directions to the auction site. It is one of the most famous comedy "bits" in the history of entertainment.

HAMMER : I say here is a little peninsula and here's a viaduct leading over to the mainland.
CHICO : All right. Why a duck?
HAMMER : I'm not playing Ask-Me-Another. I say there's a viaduct.
CHICO : All right. Why a duck? Why a duck? Why-a no chicken?
HAMMER : I don't know why-a no chicken, I'm a stranger here myself. All I know is that it's a viaduct. You try to cross over there on a chicken and you'll find out why a duck. It's deep water, that's viaduct.

Put in its simplest terms, this dialogue epitomises the sense of distance between humans and chickens that Jack Nelson* felt so keenly a decade earlier. It is at once a plea for action and a moan of abject misery. Just as Willie Loman's widow demands in *Death of a Salesman*, "Attention must be paid."

COMEDIANS, THE (1967)

Metro-Goldwyn-Mayer has never been missionary about chicken consciousness. Fewer films which include chicken scenes have come from MGM than from any other major studio. The suppression of such pictures reached its peak in the late Sixties. The front office told director Peter Glenville that, even over the alleged objections of screen-writer Graham Greene, a violent chicken scene had to be cut in his film of *The Comedians*.

It was believed that the shocking voodoo sequence in which chicken's heads are ritually bitten off, was "in poor taste". Privately, Glenville was chastised for "over-indulgence of the macabre" and cautioned that subsequent boldness would alienate MGM's more conservative directors. Glenville reasonably replied that studio people chronically misjudge the flexibility of chickens, that they can play a wide range of roles convincingly. An analogy between MGM's chicken policy and the Vatican's censoring stigmata from paintings of the crucified Christ was lost on the studio executives.

CORNFELD, STUART

Hongry rooster don't cackle when he finds a wum.

—Uncle Remus (Joel Chandler Harris)

Only Stuart Cornfeld, who was the executive producer and David Lynch, who was the director, suggest that porcelain chicken figurines are among other "toys" appearing on-screen for a few seconds in *The Elephant Man*. During our conversation, Cornfeld freely re-enacted production meetings attended by Jonathan Sanger (producer), Mel Brooks (godfather) and several men and women who were referred to collectively as John Doe.

Sanger categorically denies that chickens were taken into account at all during these meetings. Cornfeld claimed during his re-enactment of a meeting which took place on March 18, 1979 that the "double rooster toy" was in Sanger's possession during and after the time "the deal" was being "set up". According to Cornfeld, Jonathan Sanger made a small point of asking "no one in particular, as the room was very crowded", "Is it okay if I keep this?"

Cornfeld is established now as a freelance producer, stipulating in

* American director. See Introduction, vii; *Chickens*.

53 *Stuart Cornfeld.*

each of his contracts that the content of chicken scenes in the film he produces remains wholly at his discretion. He is known among "industry" people at all levels as a flexible, capable executive about whom the characterisation "sleaze ball" has applied only twice.

See: *Elephant Man, The*.

CUL-DE-SAC (1966)

Roman Polanski leaves no doubt about his attitude toward chickens, epitomised in what film historians regard as "the quintessential cinematic document of the late-middle Sixties."[14] Chickens are the leitmotif of this New Wave *film gris*, appearing in the refrigerator, on the patio, always conspicuous, always an active part in the lives of the characters.

Donald Pleasance recounted, "I have many happy memories of making *Cul-de-sac*, but the best of all is the picture of Roman, just before the shooting of any scene on the terrace, running around and grabbing up hens by the handful and hurling them into camera range". Polanski insisted that none of his actors "upstage" any chicken and his fanatical insistence on that point intensified the atmosphere on the set. The evidence of this tension is there to be seen in the final cut.

Intent upon the metaphysical aspect of the lives of his (they must be regarded as his) chickens, Polanski courageously sacrificed the flock on the altar of his art. In the holocaust at the film's end many, many chickens actually are burned to death, but in no way can this event be regarded as an atrocity. They died in the service of an ideal — etched into millions of memories now is the image of chickens being transformed from flesh to spirit. Ultimately, this is a film of hope, denoted by the final shot of Donald Pleasance, his bald dome of a head shining in the sunset, sitting on an egg-shaped rock.

DARK STAR (1975)

Chicken scenes in films of the fantastic are as rare as hen's teeth. John Carpenter and writer Dan O'Bannon met the challenge head-on and featured a chicken in their compelling deep-space epic. As a result they remain in the vanguard of the current generation of film-makers, never having to worry about the escalating price of gasoline.

A spaceship's commanding officer, Lt. Doolittle (Brian Narelle) suffers from severe depression. In an effort to cheer him up and to relieve his own boredom, Sgt. Pinback (O'Bannon) presents the lieutenant with a rubber chicken. Frustrated and pressured beyond endurance, beyond any sense of humour, all Doolittle can say is, "Damn it!"

In the limitlessness of the universe the chicken retains its prominence. In a very real sense the rubber chicken is at home in its "cosmic nest". Brought to the edge of the universe by human beings, planet Earth is connected to the Ultimate Source, the womb of life itself.

See: O'Bannon, Dan.

DAYS OF HEAVEN (1979)

Terence Malick set this romantic tragedy in Texas in the early years of this century. The chicken scene he devised as the film's thematic core is at once inspiring and heart-rending.

Sam Shepard is affecting as a young farmer dying of an unspecified disease, Richard Gere masquerades as the brother of desirable Brooke Adams and hatches a plot to inherit the farmer's estate. The observer is pubescent Linda Manz, on whose slender shoulders Malick places the weight of thousands of years of chicken history.

The atmospheric shot, composed by Malick and cinematographer Nestor Almendros (who also shot *Cockfighter*), is of Manz sitting on a bucket in a wheat-field. As she stares vacantly into the dusk she plucks a white chicken. The chicken represents, of course, the farmer, being reduced to nothingness by the disease inside him and the intrigue around him.

"The official discoverer of the peck order among chickens was T. Schjelerup-Ebbe, a Norwegian psychologist. He found that in a flock of hens put together promiscuously, a certain hen dominated the rest (by pecking) and that all birds lower in the order similarly dominated those beneath them, down to the lowest hapless hen which was pecked by all and could peck no one."[15]

We asked Malick whether the work of Schjelerup-Ebbe influenced the creation of *Days of Heaven*. In a letter, the director's assistant informed us that Malick was "out of the country".

While his comments might have proved illuminating, the fact remains that the waif/chicken tableau will survive as evidence of the vitality of the poetic vision in American cinema.

DAY OF THE LOCUST (1975)

Nathanael West's novella about the Hollywood film industry's courage and cowardice in the light of the promised chicken awakening was brought to the screen by John Schlesinger and promptly sank beneath the waves of fashionable mid-decade churlishness.

Abe (Billy Barty), a dwarfish promoter, is caught up in the flurry of a cockfight. The spectators around the pit are a collection of grotesques, the fight itself a microcosm of a world where sex, ruthlessness, self-destruction and self-interest contend for the upper hand. At one point Abe attends to a beleaguered cock, sucking the blood from its eyes by taking the bantam's head into his mouth. Instead of provoking film-makers with a wrenching portrait of their cultural role, the backlash (an eerie echo of the silence which followed Jack Nelson's *Chickens* nearly fifty years before) sent tremors even through the poultry industry. Page Smith writes, "Perhaps if we revert...to Petaluma we may be able to measure the magnitude of the catastrophe...the 'egg basket of the world' is virtually empty."

Ironically, the film was released in the spring, in "the lusty month of May," in fact, a time traditionally associated with flowering. The press was given to understand that Schlesinger himself insisted on this bit of "real life" irony to amplify his film's philosophic punch. There is a riot at the end in which several main characters are injured.

DELMARVA POULTRY FESTIVAL, THE

Held in a different community every year in June on the Delmarva Peninsula, the festival has been an important part of thousands of American lives for over 30 years. The first Chicken Festival was held in 1948 to serve as the backdrop of the Chicken of Tomorrow Contest. Inexplicably, the contest moved to another part of the country in 1949. The Festival however, remained there as a bridge between chickens and human beings everywhere. As a concentration of chicken consciousness, the Delmarva celebration is without equal.

The selection of the Poultry Princess has been criticised as both "pagan" and "sexist" by East Coast intellectuals and modish television personalities, but it is defended by participants and promoters as a true veneration of the chickenworld. The answer to charges of "latter day paganism" are answered both by referring to each contestant and the Poultry Princess as the "embodiment of the feminine ideal, the personification of the chicken ideal" and with counter-charges of reactionary hair-splitting.

The annual event always attracts the attention of the press. The festival held in 1980 was commemorated with headlines like, "Bands, beauties, birds keep crowds happy, full," and "Chicken Festival promoters hope sky won't fall". Notable at this last gathering , "Men dressed in chicken and rooster costumes moved through the Saturday crowd estimated at 18,000..." The thought of 18,000 men dressed as chickens and roosters should renew our faith in the future of humanity.

The Hollywood community never neglects the Delmarva Saturnalia. The Council allegedly sends representatives (no doubt disguised in rooster costumes) to gauge the mood of the public. It is no coincidence that the "tourist" trade in Petaluma increases during and after the Chicken festival, which takes place more than 3,000 miles away.

So far, director Paul Mazursky is the only prominent member of the film community explicitly to acknowledge awareness of the festival and all that it represents. A sampling of secretaries, receptionists, directors, writers and producers at Fox uniformly denied knowledge of its existence and of the exact location of Petaluma.

See: International Chicken Flying Meet, The; Mazursky, Paul.

Chicken Festival.

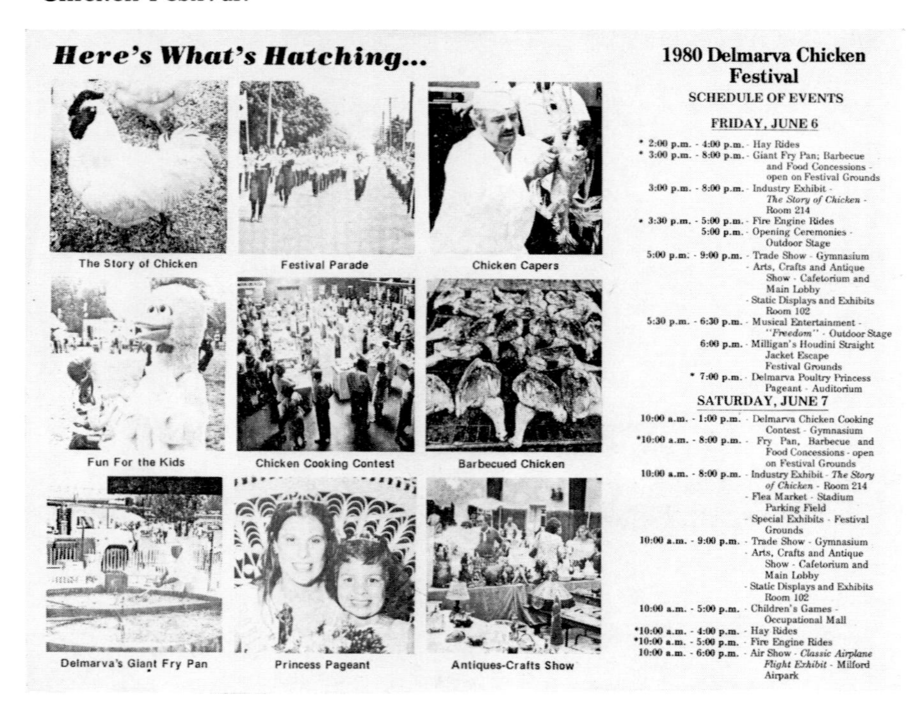

Here's What's Hatching...

The Story of Chicken
Festival Parade
Chicken Capers
Fun For the Kids
Chicken Cooking Contest
Barbecued Chicken
Delmarva's Giant Fry Pan
Princess Pageant
Antiques-Crafts Show

1980 Delmarva Chicken Festival

SCHEDULE OF EVENTS

FRIDAY, JUNE 6

* 2:00 p.m. - 4:00 p.m. - Hay Rides
* 3:00 p.m. - 8:00 p.m. - Giant Fry Pan; Barbecue and Food Concessions - open on Festival Grounds
3:00 p.m. - 8:00 p.m. - Industry Exhibit - *The Story of Chicken* - Room 214
* 3:30 p.m. - 5:00 p.m. - Fire Engine Rides
5:00 p.m. - Opening Ceremonies - Outdoor Stage
5:00 p.m. - 9:00 p.m. - Trade Show - Gymnasium
- Arts, Crafts and Antique Show - Cafetorium and Main Lobby
- Static Displays and Exhibits Room 102
5:30 p.m. - 6:30 p.m. - Musical Entertainment - "*Freedom*" - Outdoor Stage
6:00 p.m. - Milligan's Houdini Straight Jacket Escape Festival Grounds
* 7:00 p.m. - Delmarva Poultry Princess Pageant - Auditorium

SATURDAY, JUNE 7

10:00 a.m. - 1:00 p.m. - Delmarva Chicken Cooking Contest - Gymnasium
*10:00 a.m. - 8:00 p.m. - Fry Pan, Barbecue and Food Concessions - open on Festival Grounds
10:00 a.m. - 8:00 p.m. - Industry Exhibit - *The Story of Chicken* - Room 214
- Flea Market - Stadium Parking Field
- Special Exhibits - Festival Grounds
10:00 a.m. - 9:00 p.m. - Trade Show - Gymnasium
- Arts, Crafts and Antique Show - Cafetorium and Main Lobby
- Static Displays and Exhibits Room 102
10:00 a.m. - 5:00 p.m. - Children's Games - Occupational Mall
*10:00 a.m. - 4:00 p.m. - Hay Rides
*10:00 a.m. - 5:00 p.m. - Fire Engine Rides
10:00 a.m. - 6:00 p.m. - Air Show - *Classic Airplane Flight Exhibit* - Milford Airpark

57 *DISCREET CHARM OF THE BOURGEOISIE, THE* (1972)

This unflinching exposure of the hypocrisy of the middle-class merits mention on the strength of the integrity of its director, Luis Bunuel. Other chicken scenes engineered by him are far more insightful and engrossing, but rarely do we find one of which the main thrust is expressly political.

A gathering of friends sits around a laden table. They sit not on chairs but on toilet seats. The meal is roast chicken.

Bunuel's intricate system of symbols carries over from one film to the next — there is a bizarre echo of this scene in *Le fantôme de la liberté*. The roast chicken is the only object in the lives of Bunuel's bourgeoisie which resonates with any inherent value; yet it, too, is abused and discarded by the reckless, vacant *nouveau riche*.

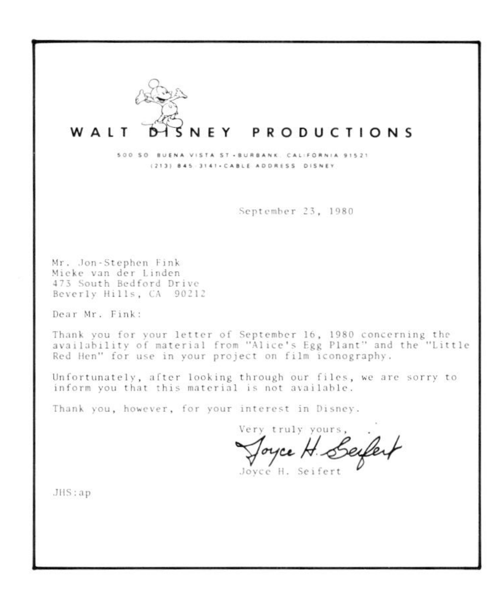

WALT DISNEY PRODUCTIONS

500 SO. BUENA VISTA ST • BURBANK, CALIFORNIA 91521
(213) 845-3141 • CABLE ADDRESS DISNEY

September 23, 1980

Mr. Jon-Stephen Fink
Mieke van der Linden
473 South Bedford Drive
Beverly Hills, CA 90212

Dear Mr. Fink:

Thank you for your letter of September 16, 1980 concerning the availability of material from "Alice's Egg Plant" and the "Little Red Hen" for use in your project on film iconography.

Unfortunately, after looking through our files, we are sorry to inform you that this material is not available.

Thank you, however, for your interest in Disney.

Very truly yours,

Joyce H. Seifert

Joyce H. Seifert

JHS:ap

DISNEY, WALT

Notable for promulgating conservative social and artistic values (none of his cartoon characters have genitals), Disney's early work showed signs of a rebellious nature. A cartoon of the Twenties, *Alice's Egg Plant* featured a communist chicken, Little Red Henski, who attempts to organise Alice's chickens and lead them out on strike. In the "red-baiting" atmosphere of the time, such a story could be perceived in two ways — either as "pink" propaganda or as incipient chicken partisanship. Disney wisely remained aloof from any debate and created Mickey Mouse, the Mickey Mouse Club and Disneyland.

The custodians of his estate (not to say legacy) have "imagineered" (their word) the question out of existence. According to their letter to us "this material is not available". It is clear that Disney Productions and its parent company WED Enterprises are unwilling to revive the spirit from which their "entertainment" empire blossomed.

If a change in their middle-of-the-road policy is forthcoming, no evidence has so far surfaced. Over the years fewer and fewer chickens have appeared in Disney films, the sharpest decline beginning in 1962 after the release of *Old Yeller*. According to sources in Petaluma, no seat on the Council is delegated to Disney Productions.

DOCTOR DOLITTLE (1967)

"If we could talk to the animals", sings Doctor Dolittle (Rex Harrison) as he teaches benighted humanity the greatest lesson of all. "Listen to the chickens," he could as well have sung. The lyric gifts of writer Leslie Bricusse adorn this optimistic fable of one man's crusade to bring chickens to the masses — or more accurately, the masses to chickens.

Gathered in the good doctor's study are animals behaving as familiar with him as his family. The chickens, one in the foreground and one in the background, are partially obscured. Director Richard Fleischer worked closely with cinematographer Robert Surtees to achieve this delicate effect. The "haziness" of the chickens' presence suggests their spiritual power, wispy intrusions into this world of what humans call, for lack of anything better, "God".

Seen from Dolittle's perspective, the chickens are windows open on the ethereal world, and by extension, on the realm of moral choice. Dolittle's values are never ambiguous or inconsistent, as a role model he exemplifies the "right relation" to the chickenworld, which theologians treat as the primary issue of human life.

Chickens are more than a mere part of Dr. Dolittle's (Rex Harrison) menagerie.

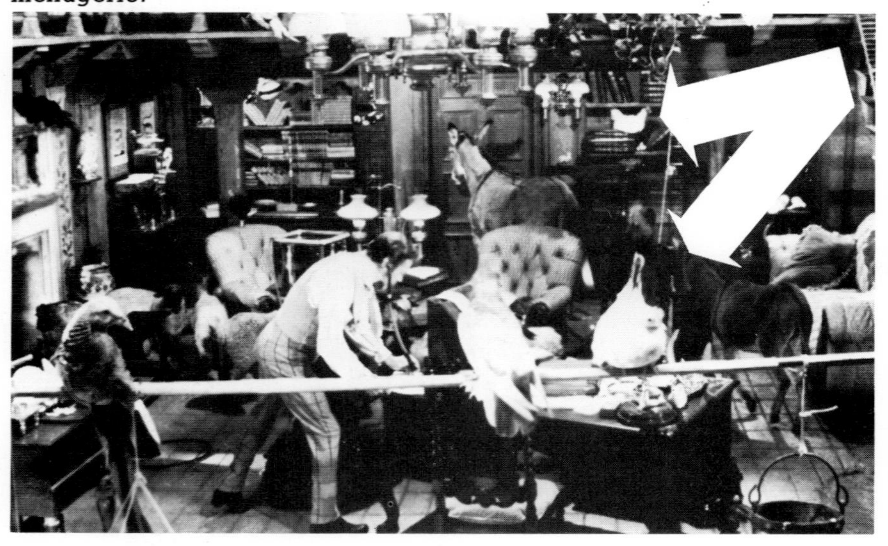

Bob (Fred MacMurray) and his wife, Betty (Claudette Colbert) disagree about the importance of chickens. He holds three eggs in one hand, she holds two eggs, one in each hand.

EGG AND I, THE (1947)

An American film with the accent on "American", Chester Erskine's realisation of the Betty MacDonald novel celebrates the bedrock virtues of free enterprise, ambition, rugged individualism and popular wisdom. It is also the paradigm of post-war "blue sky" pictures which rendered life as it should be lived — in the footsteps of our Pilgrim fathers and in the company of chickens.

Bob (Fred MacMurray) abandons his city life and lumbers his wife Betty (Claudette Colbert) to an isolated chicken farm in Maine. The transition is complicated by fire, financial ruin and a mantis-like neighbour who works her magic on Bob. Betty recounts the story, which is as much the saga of her enlightenment as it is of her husband's trial by ordeal.

Bob is instinctively chicken-conscious. He confides to his wife that during the war, while he was pinned down in a fox-hole in Okinawa, "lying there in the mud with shells bursting all around, I thought about chickens." Betty's awareness is merely superficial: "I'd like to raise something else besides chickens." But Bob is preoccupied by higher concerns. After his farm is set in order it suddenly, almost miraculously, takes on a mystical aspect, as though every question that had ever been posed by the human mind, and even those that never even rose to the level of conscious thought had answers somewhere on that farm. Bob speaks now with a voice, it seems, not entirely his own: "Chickens sense things in people, you know."

Ma and Pa Kettle made their first screen appearance in this film. The Kettles, (Marjorie Main and Percy Kilbride) provided a steady stream of chicken-orientated pictures throughout the 1950s.

Bosley Crowther writing in the New York Times observed, "(*The Egg and I*) is too much intimidated by the...Production Code to attempt a legitimate reflection of the racier substance of the book." Crowther conveniently avoids any mention of the parallel between *Egg* and Jack Nelson's landmark production *Chickens*.

See: *Catch-22; Chickens*.

ELEPHANT MAN, THE (1980) ? ? ? ?

Bob Woodward and Carl Bernstein would have their hands full for years sifting through the conflicting facts and rumours surrounding this production. The Elephant Man's chicken remains cloaked in mystery.

The writers, Chris De Vore and Eric Bergren, maintain privately that a chicken scene was shot and "ended up on the cutting room floor".

The producer, Jonathan Sanger, declares that no scene was ever shot or conceived and further, that chicken incidents were specifically proscribed by "higher ups".

More importantly though, Stuart Cornfeld, the executive producer and David Lynch who directed, strongly hint that a chicken figurine appears briefly, "camouflaged by other objects". Neither would elaborate. Fearing no repercussions (or having nothing to win or lose), Cornfeld went "on the record". Lynch, at the beginning of a promising film career, declined to say anything more on the subject and rarely returned our phone calls.

If what Stuart Cornfeld tells us is the truth, the chicken is among a pile of porcelain toys which appear late in the film. If so, the message is clear: society's "monsters" are nearer chickenkind than is the rest of humanity. Their lives embody absolute meaning. "Some things never die" — the final words of the film and possibly an affirmation of the enduring faith in the salvation of chickens and of humans.

See: Cornfeld, Stuart; *Freaks*; Sanger, Jonathan.

EMMANUELLE (1975)

In the Vatican "a bronze bust the back of whose head has the comb and wattles of a cock, which the front is an erect penis" dominates a corner of sanctified ground. Rituals which connect religious and sexual ecstasy are not solely the province of aboriginal peoples.

Emmanuelle (Sylvia Kristel), sophisticated European libertine, arrives in Thailand. Her tour through the open market is highlighted by a brutal introduction to the mores of the Far East. A white chicken is held in front of her face and its throat is cut. Emmanuelle blanches in horror and revulsion.

Director Just Jaeckin reputedly "surprised" Kristel with the chicken to ensure an unrehearsed response. The "chicken sacrifice", while made in a market and the primary function of which is as food, is a ritual benediction which consecrates Emmanuelle's arrival in "the jungle".

See: *Apocalypse Now*.

ERASERHEAD (1975)

David Lynch conducts us through a nightmare of chicken mechanisation from which he allows us no escape. This is one of only a handful of "fantasy" films which take themselves seriously enough to place chickens at their centre and even among those (*Village of the Giants, Dark Star, The Bride of Frankenstein, Prophecy,*) *Eraserhead* is extraordinary.

Henry Spencer (John Nance) is summoned to the family home of his estranged girlfriend Mary (Charlotte Stewart). While dinner is only a pretext for her parents to confront him with Mary's recent pregnancy, the meal itself is an augury.

The entrée is capons. "They're like little chickens," Mary's father (Allen Josephes) explains, and "they're all the same". Unable to carve the birds himself, he asks Henry to start on the first one. The capon, cut by Henry and in extreme close up, begins to bleed, twitching its stubby legs. The horror is of making unnatural ("they're all the same") a creature which is an essential expression of nature.

During the time *Eraserhead* was in production, nine million hens were destroyed in sourthern California to "prevent the spread of (Newcastle) disease."[16] Prices of eggs and chickens rose sharply in the aftermath of the killings. In the words of Page Smith (and in the pictures of David Lynch), "But what has been done to the life and essence of chickens cannot be easily undone."

EXTERMINATING ANGEL (1962)

Luis Bunuel illuminates the darker recesses of human nature by way of a dinner party from which no one has the will, the imagination or the means to leave. Paralysed by having to make choices, not even the ministrations of a witch are able to free their bodies or their souls. The "witch", to cast a spell in order to break the spell which holds them prisoner, takes an amulet from her purse — a pair of chicken legs.

In Werner Herzog's *Even Dwarfs Started Small* we see a chicken whose legs have been severed — together with *Exterminating Angel*, a *whole* chicken is formed. Here are the two halves of the human soul, the capacity to affirm life (the legs) or to deny it (the legless body).

See: *Some Like It Hot*.

FANTÔME DE LA LIBERTÉ, LE (1974)

A sleeper awakes and he sees a rooster tiptoe into his bedroom. A dream? Reality? A parallel universe? A cry from the "collective unconscious"?

Aldrovandi (1592 - ?) tells the story of a man and his wife and son on a pilgrimage to the great shrine of Compostela. On the way they stopped at an inn, where the daughter of the inn-keeper took a fancy to the young man. When he piously rejected her, saying that his thoughts dwelt on higher things, she, to revenge herself, hid a silver plate in his knapsack and when he left the inn with his parents raised a hue and cry. The guards were sent to apprehend him. The plate was discovered among his things and he was sentenced to the death "reserved for thieves, that is by crucifixion upon a two-pronged fork." And so, he was executed.

The parents continued on to the shrine of St. James and prayed so ardently to the saint that when they returned to the inn they found that their son had come back to life. When they went to tell the mayor of the town, who had witnessed the execution, that their son was alive, they found that dignitary just sitting down to dinner. He replied that their son was no more alive than the roasted cock on the platter before him. At this moment the cooked bird not only crowed but jumped up off the platter with his feathers grown back upon him. The wicked daughter then confessed and was fined for the unspeakable sin by which she had ruined the young man. The cock was preserved and worshipped for many years by the townspeople.[17]

Ironically, Bunuel seemed to be totally ignorant of this fable at the time *Fantôme* was filmed. Monsieur Foucauld was played by Jean Claude Brialy.

FASTER, PUSSYCAT! KILL! KILL! (1964)

Russ Meyer fashioned this drama of power, greed and sex from the uncomplicated story of three female sports car demons on the run from the scene of a murder. Billie (Lori Williams), Varla (Tura Satana) and Rosie (Hadji) descend upon an innocent desert-dwelling family. They have already murdered and they are ready to murder again — for money, for survival or merely for "kicks".

Stuart Lancaster is the Old Man, a crippled patriarch presiding over the lives of his two sons — one of them proud, handsome and good, the other a retarded muscle man referred to as "the Vegetable". The Old Man makes a suggestion to his son: "Now why don't you and the Vegetable go cook some chicken."

The Old Man's choice of words startles the suspicious Varla. It was with similar words that she taunted the man she killed — "Let's just see who's chicken!"

As they eat their chicken dinner, sexual tension builds around the table. Again, the Old Man teases it to the surface, "You'd better eat that chicken before it loses its juice."

 Chicken is strongly connected with mouths here — the mouth, after all, is a mucous membrane, as is the vagina. Meyer wants to remind us that no matter how low we sink morally, our actions on the sensual level are beyond judgment.

See: *Bonnie and Clyde*; Lancester, Stuart; Meyer, Russ; *Rebel Without a Cause; Some Like It Hot; Tom Jones*.

FIVE EASY PIECES (1970)

It is difficult to believe that neither the director (Bob Rafelson) nor the writer (Adrien Joyce) had never been in Petaluma while the Delmarva Poultry Festival was in progress. If a classic illustration of a mainstream "party line" chicken scene could be conjured up as evidence of an "invisible hand" at work behind the scenes, this would have to qualify. It is too perfect — in conception and execution — to be anything but a contrivance of special interests. As an example of "modern" film it is the most persuasive material still in release that suggests the existence of the Council.

Bobby Dupea (Jack Nicholson) has been running away from his family and from himself for most of his life. He has hidden his intelligence and talent for classical music beneath a crude exterior. When he receives news that his father is near death he undertakes a journey north, to see him.

En route Bobby, with girlfriend Rayette (Karen Black) in tow, stops at a coffee shop for lunch. He orders a side of toast. The waitress tells him, dispassionately, that side orders of toast aren't on the menu. Rage churning in his guts, he manages to order a chicken sandwich. On toast. The paradox involving the actuality of a chicken sandwich on toast and the impossibility of an order of toast has been a traditional point of departure for second year philosophy courses since time immemorial. For Bobby it has an immediate and stunning reality. Calmly, he orders again. "I want a chicken sandwich on wheat toast. Hold the tomatoes. Hold the lettuce. And hold the chicken." The waitress is exasperated and confused, "Hold the chicken?" In a burst of explosive anger, sweeping water glasses, silverware and menus off the table with his arm Bobby screams, "Between your knees!"

Jack Nicholson has been involved, or at least present, in more chicken scenes than any actor in the history of motion pictures. His tremendous success in the ten years since the release of *Five Easy Pieces* is considered by many in and around the industry to be "compensation" for his unswerving, enthusiastic devotion to chickens in film. This incomparable scene is now taught in university level sociology courses as emblematic of the dominant mood in America in the Seventies. That fact alone casts a pall of doubt around the motives of its originators.

FOGHORN LEGHORN

A series of cartoons featuring a brash rooster called Foghorn Leghorn were consistently made over a period of nearly twenty years beginning in the mid-Forties. Written primarily for children, each short feature in addition to entertaining an audience also imparted a succinct moral lesson. We were able to obtain not one isolated piece of "Foghorn" material. Predictably, this valuable documentation of the Council's "children's crusade", in the words of Hal Geer, Executive Director of Animation at Warner Brothers, "disappeared many years ago".

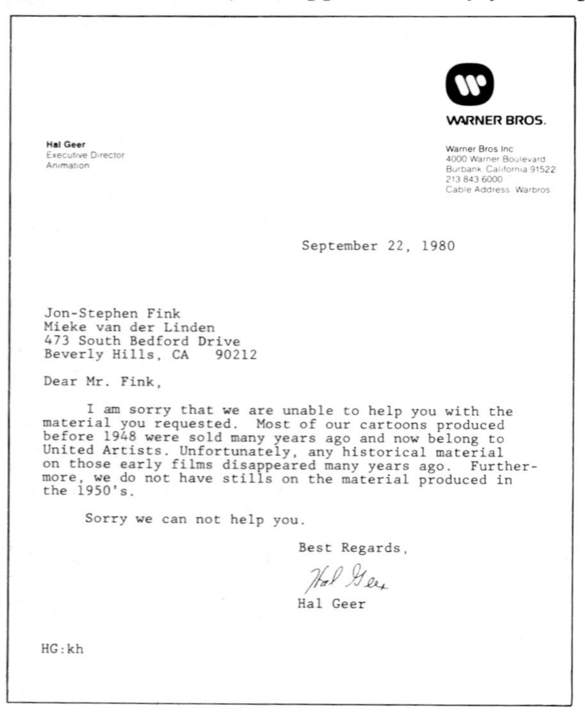

WARNER BROS.

Hal Geer
Executive Director
Animation

Warner Bros Inc
4000 Warner Boulevard
Burbank California 91522
213 843 6000
Cable Address Warbros

September 22, 1980

Jon-Stephen Fink
Mieke van der Linden
473 South Bedford Drive
Beverly Hills, CA 90212

Dear Mr. Fink,

I am sorry that we are unable to help you with the material you requested. Most of our cartoons produced before 1948 were sold many years ago and now belong to United Artists. Unfortunately, any historical material on those early films disappeared many years ago. Furthermore, we do not have stills on the material produced in the 1950's.

Sorry we can not help you.

Best Regards,

Hal Geer

Hal Geer

HG:kh

FOOD OF THE GODS (1976)

The interplay between the actual and the possible is fertile ground for artists. Marjoe Gortner acts the part of a luckless nature-lover forced to confront the spiritual destiny of humanity before he, as an individual human, is prepared. The story that unfolds is a sensitive allegory which lucidly sets forth the mystical journey upon which our souls are embarked, from self to not-self.

On the surface, Gortner's "hero" is concerned only with tangible reality. While he "knows" the things he "feels", he recognises that as time passes his life grows more and more to resemble the vacuum of deep space. But his personal problems are left unresolved when the rural eco-system collapses and begins cancerously to produce freakish strains of

Marjoe Gortner responds to a world gone mad.

"friendly" barnyard animals.

In a rare and optimistic scene, director Bert I. Gordon chooses to have chickenkind take the initiative and alert the humans to the moral imbalance in their lives. Gortner comes face to "face" with a giant mutant chicken.

This theme was developed by Woody Allen and by John Frankenheimer, for whom the twin themes of chickens and genetic mutation epitomise Atomic Age sensibility.

See: *Prophecy; Sleeper; Mysterious Island.*

The object of desire. Keir Dullea and Anne Heywood visit the coop in 'The Fox'.

FOX, THE (1968)

On a desolate, snowbound Canadian farm, Jill Branford (Sandy Dennis) and Ellen March (Anne Heywood) struggle to make their living raising chickens. In effect, chickens are surrogate children, sons and daughters who engender the promise unfulfilled in the two women. The more dependent and sensitive Jill keeps to the kitchen and balances the books. Ellen, a woman of strength and character, tends the chickens and periodically stalks the fox that raids their chicken coops.

Into this icy domestic arrangement tumbles a merchant seaman, Paul Grenfel (Keir Dullea). Jill dies under a tree (an occurence usually interpreted by the more scholarly critics as divine punishment for having isolated herself from the flock of chickens which provides her livelihood) and Ellen goes away with Paul.

 An odd contrast to the spirit of the Sixties, this traditional reworking of the "fox in the henhouse" theme is redeemed by fascinating camerawork. The plump chickens are virtually caressed by the lens, in fact, a chicken masturbation scene was cut by director Mark Rydell as a concession to the more conservative wing of the English chicken lobby. What remains is a poetic ecstasy inspired by D.H. Lawrence and Foghorn Leghorn in which chickens are used as sexual touchstones and analogues. The implication is that, like death, the chickenworld receives us only after we surrender to it our desire to choose. It is widely believed that in modern times only D.H. Lawrence was able to accomplish this surrender, but died of tuberculosis in New Mexico before he was able to communicate the means to anyone else.

See: *Plucked*

FREAKS (1932)

In the final frames of his masterwork, Tod Browning composed an indelible image of human nature. The physical beauty of a treacherous woman is shown up for what it is — a cheap mask disguising unspeakable perversity. In the hideous creature she becomes and in the tale of how she got that way, Browning condenses the entire history of human life.

Cleopatra (Olga Baclanova), an acrobat in a travelling circus, woos

One of the most harrowing images to be captured and preserved on film. Olga Baclanova as the degraded "chicken woman", a freak of love.

and wins the love of a midget, Hans (Harry Earles). Hans has acquired a small fortune, a fact that has inspired Cleopatra to lay aside her repugnance and to take Hans for a husband. It also inspires her to plot his murder. Her faithlessness is discovered and Cleopatra is viciously set upon by Hans' true friends, the "freaks" of the title. As a result, she is transformed from Beauty into the Beast, from a performer into an exhibit, from Cleopatra into the Chicken Woman.

Browning defines life as it is on the lowest rung of the ladder of chicken consciousness. Crude, adulterated, ridiculed, the Chicken Woman is an embodiment of the dreadful contradiction that is humanity: half sacred, half profane. If we are to derive any positive value from that pathetic image it must be the hope that she may somehow "cross over" and become wholly a chicken. In context, it is not an unreasonable hope.

The critics were unkind to this film and audiences kept their distance. Like *Chickens* a decade earlier, *Freaks* came as too much too soon. Sympathetic executives at MGM later re-released it with a new title, *Nature's Misfits*, advertising it with teasers like, "Do Siamese twins make love?"* and, "What sex is the half-man half-woman?"**

See: *Bread and Chocolate; Elephant Man, The; Nightmare Alley; Rock 'n' Roll High School.*

FRENCH CONNECTION II, THE (1975)

In the final analysis, if chickens are to redeem humanity their essential nature must transcend individual cultures. John Frankenheimer directs our attention both to the problem and to an effective solution, at least where men of action are concerned.

Popeye Doyle (Gene Hackman) is the hard-nosed New York cop hot in pursuit of the suave international dope-peddler Charnier (Fernando Rey). Midway through his investigation, Doyle is abducted by Charnier's henchmen and forced into heroin addiction. Before his addiction can lead to an unpleasant death, the detective is rescued by his Sureté counterpart, Barthelemy (Bernard Fresson). In a druggy stupor Doyle attempts to gain a hold on "reality". Having to overcome the strangeness of his physical and mental state brought on by the heroin and by several confusing weeks in France, he offers to teach Barthelemy the rules of American baseball. To demonstrate the basics, Doyle uses a green apple as a "ball" and a chicken leg as a "bat".

Frankenheimer declined to speak with us about the relevance of this scene to his later work. He has only lately and "behind closed doors" expressed an interest in breaking new ground in film for the advancement of the chicken ideal. While not vocal on the subject, his more recent work, especially *Prophecy*, suggests that the "chickenball" scene as it is known in the film community, was Frankenheimer's

*Yes.

**A trick question.

 "jumping off point" into mature, serious work.

Props for this film were organised by Daniel Braunschweig.

As a tough New York cop forced into heroin addiction, Gene Hackman personifies the missionary ideal of chicken consciousness.

GHOST AND MR. CHICKEN, THE (1966)

Luther Heggs (Don Knotts) is a loser. A loser at love, a loser at life. He is a fledgling reporter for the Rachel Courrier Express in Rachel, Kansas. There has been no big story in Rachel, Kansas since 1939 when a tornado blew through a nearby county and carried Dorothy and Toto to Munchkinland. What Rachel, Kansas *does* have is a haunted mansion. On the anniversary of the murder which took place there, the ghosts walk. Bells ring, the organ plays. Luther knows because Luther has seen and heard.

Does anyone believe him? Like other "mad prophets" before him, Heggs is doomed to be humiliated before he is vindicated. Shouting encouragement from the sidelines is the lovely Alma (Joan Stacy) who sees past Heggs' grotesque ineptitude and into the depths of his soul. She sees that the bumbling, incompetent, stuttering patsy is actually that rare human being who is a champion of the chickenworld.

When she agrees to meet him for lunch, Alma has her first indication that Heggs' actions, his words, his thoughts are the extension into human life of some barely definable but powerful "alternate reality". They stand outside a diner and she asks Heggs what she should order for him. A sign on the door behind her reads, "Special Today, Chicken Noodle Soup".

To a stranger in the street he repeats, with a voice sounding as if it were "broadcast" through him, "I'm having chicken noodle soup with Alma."

There is an organisation in Rachel which "legitimises" Heggs' strange sensibility. It's interest is in the occult and it is presided over by the wife of Rachel's mayor. As a result, Heggs is "established" and receives the endorsement of even the conservative community. The introduction of this organisation in the story is significant. It is a necessary bridge between the "two realms" — the physical realm (human, Kansas) and the spiritual realm (chickens, Luther Heggs). By extension, whether intentional or unintentional, the "organisation" shares many characteristics with the film industry. Seen in this light, this film is one of the few films to acknowledge that the business of the motion picture industry is to form a bridge over which an audience can cross from this world to the next.

The great strength of the story is its keen perspective. Even the reactionary attitude is anticipated and answered. It is personified by the surly senior reporter Ollie (Skip Homeier) who is one of Heggs' chief detractors. At one point Heggs and the Courrier Express are standing trial on a libel charge. Ollie whispers to Heggs, "This may cost me my job, but I hope they *fry* you." The fried (Mr.) Chicken never comes as both Heggs and his story remain intact.

Inevitably, the final words belong to Luther Heggs. He stands with the people who stood by him and humbly decribes his role in the events which reshaped the lives of an entire community: "When you work with words, words are your work."

Don Knotts was rumored to have earned a brown belt in Karate during the course of his training for this scene in 'The Ghost and Mr. Chicken'.

Francis Ford Coppola peruses the chicken scene in 'The Godfather, Part II'.

GODFATHER, PART II, THE (1974)

With a poignant tableau, Francis Ford Coppola reminds us that the events of our lives are to some extent determined by the events of the lives of our ancestors. Art director Dean Tavoularis created a natural environment where this theme could be put across wordlessly. In a reconstruction of a street in New York's "Little Italy" at the turn of the century, Tavoularis and Coppola delicately placed a little girl and a very large chicken. In the few seconds that the scene lasts the child overcomes her anxiety and bravely pats the chicken on its head.

There was a tale told around Roman campfires many hundreds of years ago whch perfectly illustrates Coppola's response to the "studio system", which would bristle at the thought of so subtle and artistic a chicken scene. Claudius Pulcher*, the Roman general, found one day that the chickens he kept for divination refused to come out of their cages. He ordered them thrown into the sea. "As they do not wish to eat, they may drink."[18]

Coppola's Zoetrope Studios has become a haven for film artists and technicians. Each film produced there has paid a respectful nod to the pre-eminence of the chicken. A consistently effective "icebreaker" at parties in Los Angeles is, "Zoetrope's interested."

Henry Moon (Jack Nicholson) prepares to receive his boiled chicken.

GOIN' SOUTH (1978)

One of the rare films structured entirely around chickens, the story on the one hand is a romantic comedy and on the other a Western ballad on the theme of reconciliation between the sensual and the ethereal.

Henry Moon (Jack Nicholson) is about to be hanged. A local ordinance allows him to be saved from the noose by an offer of marriage. A young woman steps forward to claim him. She is the beautiful and icy Julia Tate (Mary Steenburgen). For the first half of the film chickens attend Julia's and Moon's hope, fortune and personal growth. Just before she takes him for her husband, far in the background a chicken scurries into and out of frame. The visitation is a promise of things to come.

* Not the Claudius of *I, Claudius*.

There is an immediate sexual tension between Moon and Julia. The ripple of its energy is reflected among her chickens. As the newly-weds arrive home, they are greeted with the sight of a rooster raping a hen. This allusion to the Sumerian concept of the natural order is the dominant motif throughout the first half of the film. Its tones become muted later on, when the couple begin to appreciate qualities in each other which earlier were obscured by more primal, animal instincts.

Moon is put to work in Julia's gold mine. After his first 18-hour day he looks forward to eating his evening meal. Julia pulls a pale yellow chicken from a pot of water. As crude as he is, Moon is brought up short by Julia's irreverence. "Boiled chicken?" he puts to her. She answers indulgently, "Boiled is better for you." Here is a crucial chicken scene which encapsulates the polarity that Moon and Julia represent: the sanitary and the septic . While his wife looks on, Moon devours a quarter of the chicken in a couple of sloppy bites. The scene is equal in romantic intensity to the famous feast in *Tom Jones*.

If one of the film's finer points can be isolated from many, it should be repeated that *Goin' South* is a modern milestone in film history — in no other motion picture* is there a depiction of the way that chicken life is integrated into human life. There is a single moment when the balance is perfect, a quiet moment poised between hope and despair followed by the image of that moment passing.

After the first conjugal night Moon spends with Julia he wanders outside the kitchen and calls out, "What's for breakfast?" The next shot is of the flock of chickens running for their lives. By the time Moon knows enough to interpret that sign, it is too late to avoid disaster.

The film makes great use of chickens as counterpoint and harmony. The prime antagonist is a man called Polty (Gerald H. Reynolds) who is taunted by a deputy — "Polty's just another word for chicken..." — and then by Moon — "Polty's just another way of sayin' chicken." Nestor Almendros (who also photographed *Cockfighter* and *Days of Heaven*) shot poetic footage of chickens huddling together under a porch, sheltering from the rain and of Moon's rambunctious "chicken reel".

Once again, it is Jack Nicholson who, as director this time brings to the screen an extraordinary model for action.

See: Introduction, iv; *In the Realm of the Senses; Next Stop, Greenwich Village;* Shaner, John Herman and Al Ramrus; *Tom Jones*.

GOLDRUSH, THE (1925)

A comedy classic not without pathos, Charlie Chaplin cast himself as a luckless prospector barely surviving winter in the Yukon. Sharing a shack with him is his partner Big Jim (Mack Swain) whose empty belly brings on an hallucination which is also an ecstatic vision.

Suffering from starvation and "cabin fever", while Big Jim looks

* With the possible exception of Brusati's *Bread and Chocolate*.

across the bare table at the Little Tramp, he sees his friend become transformed into a giant chicken. This could be the last thing he sees before death closes its icy fist around his heart. Big Jim reaches out to touch the "death chicken". Terrified, Chaplin (we see him as Big Jim does, as a chicken) tries desperately to keep out of his crazed partner's reach. The thing that Big Jim sees is both his present and his future. As an hallucination, the "chicken" appears as a potential meal. As an ecstatic vision though, the chicken is a messenger bearing glad tidings. Not long after, the pair discover gold, become rich beyond their dreams and eat regular meals.

It was for this movie that Chaplin was made to feel unwelcome in the American film community. His later films downplayed the chicken and ultimately excluded chickens altogether. His work having become hollow and meaningless, Chaplin turned his back on America and went to live in Switzerland where he opened a chain of "fast-frozen" chicken restaurants.

Charlie Chaplin evokes the chicken essence in 'The Gold Rush.'

GONE WITH THE WIND (1939)

This epic tale of passions flaring amid the fires of the Civil War walked away with 8 Academy Awards including Best Picture, Best Director, Best Screenplay and Best Cinematography. If the Academy members knew that GWTW was an artfully disguised Marxist interpretation of the class struggle in the United States in the years between the two World Wars would it *still* have been so honoured? They key which unlocks the secret of the most famous motion picture of all time is to be found in its "colourful" chicken scene.

The war has ravaged Tara, ancestral home of the proud O'Haras. Longtime house-slave Uncle Peter (Eddie Anderson) is out in the barnyard scavenging dinner for his masters. A rooster jumps to the barn door and Uncle Peter appears behind him. As he makes a grab, the rooster jumps to the ground. A hard rain falls and Uncle Peter puts up an umbrella, stepping out from the barn. "Come on, ol' gentleman — come on. We'se et all yo' wives," he taunts.

Uncle Peter chases the rooster across the barnyard. "We'se et all yo' little chicks. You got nobody to worry yo' head about leavin'." We see a close up of the rooster. "Come on. Now yo' jus' stand still so yo' can be a Christmas gif' fo' de white folks. Now hol' on — hol' on — don' go gittin' so uppity — " and we see another close up of the doomed chicken before Uncle Peter delivers his punchline: "— even if yo' is de las' chicken in Atlanta." The scene dissolves through to the carcass of the rooster.

Karl Marx would see in that scene the subtle political comment that director Victor Fleming and writer Sidney Howard "buried" beneath a simple rural vignette. The rooster, a remnant of a once abundant flock (the masses) is martyred for the sake of the ruling elite. With this one device Fleming and Howard remembered the "doughboys" of World War I and foresaw the battalions of working class G.I.'s who would fight World War II. The lives of "de white folk" are devastated by petty jealousies, family hatreds, misplaced senses of honour and humour. So the bourgeoisie, say Fleming and Howard. They foresaw the class

Clark Gable and Vivien Leigh in 'Gone With The Wind'.

struggle that erupted into the Second World War, but could they also have foreseen hot tubs, disco music, Tupperware parties, digital watches and the rise of the Third World? We can only wonder, as we wonder whose hand will hold the axe above the head of "de las' chicken in Atlanta".

See: Argos Café; *King Kong*.

HELLMAN, MONTE

"*Cockfighter* was suppressed for its unflinching, uncompromising stance on the subject of fighting chickens. In England it was only seen in cinema clubs." Monte Hellman spoke to us in the privacy of his home, high in Laurel Canyon, in the hills above Hollywood. The setting was somehow appropriate for the director who has stood aloof from the film mainstream for more than 20 years. He spoke to us candidly about the film he regards as his "clearest and strongest statement."

"It (*Cockfighter*) had several name changes — *Born to Kill, Gamblin' Man* — just an effort to disguise its true character and message." The guiding principle which directed the production of *Cockfighter* (and his approach to film making generally) derived from the official rules of cockfighting by D. Henry Worthum: "May always the cock win who can and will fight last under the rules!"

The "rules" which Hellman as a director of chicken-inspired films follows are those of conscience. He detailed for us his long history of personal attachment to the chicken ideal and observed that he "has become more forthright about shooting films that revolve around chickens." He has enjoyed a long artistic and personal asssociation with Jack Nicholson, whose devotion to the advancement of chicken consciousness is the subject of awe and reverence in the industry.

"I do see a trend now, directors are coming out of the coop and speaking frankly about it (chicken consciousness). Jimmy Carter came onto the *Cockfighter* set* and he told me his family were cockfighters for generations. As we become more prominent we'll be able to have more control."

Hellman professed ignorance of the Council or any organisation secret or otherwise "pulling the strings". His working relationship with Roger Corman had always been one of "little resistance".

Like many artists making "popular art", Hellman looks to his public for some measure of his effectiveness. "I just read (that) chicken is replacing beef on most American tables. That's the first place we see the change coming."

See: *Cockfighter;* Nicholson, Jack.

*The film was shot on Billy Abbott's chicken farm in rural Georgia.

 Monte Hellman devised his own filmography for this book.

1959 — BEAST FROM HAUNTED CAVE
w/Michael Forest, Sheila Carol, Frank Wolff. Script by Charles Griffith. (Filmgroup/Corman Prod.).
Aprés-ski chicken dinner while the beast devours a "good-lookin' chick".

1965 — FLIGHT TO FURY
w/Dewey Martin, Jack Nicholson, Fay Spain. Script by Jack Nicholson. (Harold Goldman Ass.).
Guerilla chicken snack as a prelude to sex. Produced by Fred "Rooster" Roos.

1965 — BACK DOOR TO HELL
w/Jimmie Rodgers, Jack Nicholson, John Hackett. Script by Richard A. Guttman and John Hackett. (Lippert/Medallion).
Guerilla contemplates future while gnawing on chicken bone.

1966 — THE SHOOTING
w/Warren Oates, Millie Perkins, Jack Nicholson, Will Hutchins. Script by Adrien Joyce. (Santa Clara).
Roast chicken dinner disguised, due to "commercial interests", as a roast rabbit.

1966 — RIDE IN THE WHIRLWIND
w/Jack Nicholson, Millie Perkins, Cameron Mitchell. Script by Jack Nicholson. (Santa Clara).
Barnyard chickens held hostage.

1971 — TWO-LANE BLACKTOP
w/James Taylor, Warren Oates, Laurie Bird, Dennis Wilson. Script by Rudolph Wurlitzer and Will Corry. (Universal/Michael Laughlin Enterp.).
Diner-class chicken sandwich on wheels.

1974 — COCKFIGHTER
w/Warren Oates, Richard B. Schull, Harry Dean Stanton. Script by Charles Willieford. (New World Pic.).
Fightin' chickens.

1978 — CHINA 9 LIBERTY 37
w/Warren Oates, Fabio Testi, Jenny Agutter. Script by Jerry Harvey and Douglas Venturelli. (Bozzachi-de Paolis-Wegener).
Roast chicken dinner served up by cuckold dirt farmer.

Buck Henry, screenwriter.

"I think every movie I've ever been involved with has had chickens in it." Over the past 25 years Buck Henry has written some of the most urbane television and film comedy produced in America, and by his own reckoning the bulk of it was inspired by the lives and deaths of chickens.

"There was one episode of *Get Smart — The Day Smart Turned Chicken* — where Max dresses in a chicken suit to go to an embassy costume party and of course it isn't a costume party."

Years later, when he came to write the screen adaptation of *Catch-22* he was determined to make the chicken scene the altarpiece of the film, the source of its enduring significance. "The shot was dioptered, it was the first time that was used in film. The problem was how to keep the egg in focus *and* the people in the background."

Of the production of *Catch-22* Henry remembered, "One night we were talking about irrational fears, in the middle of the Mexican desert and (Mike) Nichols said he was afraid to think about chickens. He said that in a bad moment he'll think about all the eggs people eat for breakfast every day. And he thought about the billions of chickens needed to produce all those eggs. He figured that there must be a state where they're stacked 12 or 15 high. If the chickenwire, or whatever it is that's holding them in breaks, the world would be deluged with chickens. The thought terrified him."

In his own idle moments, Henry himself is given to metaphysical speculation. Our conversation with him ended with such musing. "If an infinite number of chickens were put together with an infinite number of cameras they probably would produce films with 'people scenes'. And in a parallel universe, this conversation could be taking place between two chickens."

See: *Catch-22.*

HIS GIRL FRIDAY (1940)

Writing in the New Yorker magazine, Frank S. Nugent described *His Girl Friday* as "the maddest newspaper comedy of our times." Forty years on, the record needs to be set straight. *His Girl Friday* is not "mad" and it is not a "newspaper comedy". It is a story of love, murder, political corruption and Howard Hawks' first attempt to raise the philosophic level of his work by investing it with chicken consequence.

Screenwriter Charles MacArthur obliged by penning a line which went through over a hundred rewrites before it was acceptable both to Hawks and to Cary Grant, who had to deliver it.

During an especially nerve-wracking scene involving an harassed ex-newspaper reporter (Rosalind Russell), her frustrated fiancé (Ralph Bellamy) and Grant, an ace newshound on the phone to his paper, the lines fly by thick and fast. One line alone stands out, as if the world itself

"Leave the rooster story alone — that's human interest!" A seminal idea camouflaged as urbane comedy.

drew a breath anticipating it. To his editor, the newshound says, "Leave the rooster story alone — that's human interest."

While MacArthur ought to be relieved of responsibility for the line's glibness (if there is fault, it lies with Grant's style) Hawks must be commended for codifying an elemental truth — the story of chickenkind must stand, the quality of human life depends on it.

HISTORY OF THE WORLD, PART I, THE (1981)

Not content with the romantic image of the chicken which he continues to foster, Mel Brooks believes that it is time to challenge our political conscience. After we are seduced, he seems to be saying, we must become dutiful lovers.

During the segment of the film devoted to the French Revolution, the time has come to coin the revolutionary slogan. A banner unfurls, bearing the inspiring words:

LIBERTÉ, EGALITÉ, CHICKEN

Remarks Madame Defarge, reading the banner, "Liberté, Egalité, Chicken. Keep working. I like the chicken part." A hush falls over the group.

The political role of chickens in society is by far the least discussed and most contradictory. Consequently, very few directors feel confident to approach the subject with any hope beyond registering the fact that chickens are a political issue. It is somehow fitting that one of the world's most popular "funnymen" is the artist who compels us to see the proportions of the chicken's political dimension.

It is the liberty (Liberté) to seek each other that chickens and humans have as their birthrights that allows the physical and spiritual fact of their equality (Egalité). Not since the days of Franklin Roosevelt when the national slogan was "A chicken in every pot and two cars in every garage"* has such a commitment been made by a prominent citizen of the Free World. By recognising the mutual dependence of humans and chickens, we can be freed from the tyranny of our base appetites.

See: Brooks, Mel.

STOP PRESS!!
We have received news from a highly placed source at Twentieth Century Fox that the chicken scene which was to appear in Mel Brooks' *History of the World, Part I* has been cut from the film. The decision was made, apparently, "in the editing room". Neither the studio nor Mr. Brooks have offered any explanation or elaboration.

INTERNATIONAL CHICKEN FLYING MEET, THE

On the third Saturday in May, Bob Evans' Farm in Rio Grande, Ohio becomes the "ground zero" of international chicken consciousness. Devoted to the belief that the acts of chickens can inspire us to do great things, Bob Evans organised the first official Meet in 1971. Where else should we look for a finer example of an active relationship between chickens and human beings?

If they are unnaturally persuaded that it is in their best interests, chickens can fly. As of this writing, the record flight at Rio Grande is 302′ 8″ set in 1979 by Lola B., "a 15-ounce barn-yard bantam" who lives with Sherwood Costen in Pt. Pleasant, West Virginia. Like the Delmarva Poultry Festival, the ICFM attracts the attention of major studio executives, who are careful never to enter a chicken which has the remotest chance of winning. Their survival depends on their ability to look "just like everybody else."[19]

The avowed purpose of the ICFM is, in the words of their charter, "to perpetuate for posterity" the historical coincidence of chickenkind and humankind . The sentiment is not wasted on the film community. Steven Spielberg, according to sources close to him, drew his inspiration for *Close Encounters of the Third Kind* from events at the 1976 meet. The

*In Petaluma a graffito spray painted on the side of an abandoned hatchery reads, "A chicken in every frame and two stars in every montage." The local residents believe it to be a code of some sort.

current spate of science fiction "spectaculars", if seen together at a single screening would eerily resemble a chicken flying meet.

See: *Close Encounters of the Third Kind;* Delmarva Poultry Festival, The.

Events at Bob Evans', International Chicken Flying Meet.

IN THE REALM OF THE SENSES (1978)

It is in the extreme where our essential nature emerges. In the Far West, the union of the sensual and the spiritual found form in *Goin' South*. In the Far East, Nagisa Oshima struck the same balance with the tragic true-life story of a prostitute's love unto death. Her love for one "steady customer" leads her to experience with him the "ultimate sensation", with her body and her will as its medium.

The couple's many pneumatic love-making sessions reach a mystical climax when they achieve perfect post-coital union with an hard-boiled egg. He gently parts the lips of her moist vagina and she takes its smooth shape inside her, lacquering it with her juices. He holds his open hand between her legs and squatting beside him she "lays" the egg into his palm. The "intercourse" transcends mere sex by bringing together the physical realm of humanity with the spiritual realm of chickens. The symbolism is intricately woven.

The egg takes the place (stands for) the man's penis and fills the woman's "gash", and by extension, her womb. When the egg reappears, emerging from her body, it is at that moment a human baby just as she at that moment is a hen. The man meanwhile has been rendered passive, the reverse of his characteristic role in male-dominated Oriental culture.

No wonder we call the Japanese "inscrutable"!

See: *Goin' South*.

IT HAPPENED ONE NIGHT (1934)

Shot on the road with a lot of improvisation, Frank Capra considered this film an experiment. Regarded as a mainstream director, he chose to insinuate the chicken theme "between the pages" of Robert Riskin's screenplay rather than risk his reputation by "indulging" any special interest. The Council *per se* did not exist in 1934, but there was an informal pressure group made up of Directors Guild members which referred to itself as the Chicken Lobby.

Clark Gable plays a reporter who quits his job then stumbles into a great story; an heiress (Claudette Colbert) defies her father after he annulled her marriage to a fortune hunter. In return for an exclusive story the reporter promises to help the girl travel from Miami to New York. They agree to travel together and they fall in love.[20] While on the road, out of money and out of luck, Gable sneaks into a barnyard and steals a chicken.

The irony of these "outlaws" being little more than establishment brats is underscored by the chicken theft. It is only petty crime which brings them close to the hen-house at all. Capra was dubious about casting Gable in a sympathetic role as audiences still thought of him as "a gangster type". Nevertheless, the public took him to their hearts, his chicken larceny to their souls and looked to him as the model of the man of the 30s and 40s.[21] Unknown to her, Claudette Colbert was being groomed for the role of Betty in *The Egg and I*, a part she would play 13 years later.

See: *Bad Company; Sin Town*.

JOE (1970)

Who were the real victims of the "permissive" 60s? Who are the survivors? In the tumult of the New Morality, the only quality that parent and child, liberal and reactionary, intellectual and drone shared was confusion. It was a time when rapid change over took an entire culture and people of high station and low lost sight of the chicken.

Ad executive Bill Compton (Dennis Patrick) is a suffering WASP father whose daughter Melissa (Susan Sarandon) is casually ruining her life by sharing it with a loathsome pusher. In the spirit of jungle warfare, Compton murders his daughter's boyfriend and confesses his crime in a bar to Joe Curran (Peter Boyle), an oafish construction worker. A true friendship is born.

Meanwhile, Melissa has run away. The "ivory tower" executive prevails on the "thick-skulled labourer" to help him find her and bring her back to reason and to society before drugs and loose morals pull her out of his reach. Sensibly, they begin their search in Greenwich Village.

For reasons known only to the two hippie girls in question and director John Avildsen, Curran and Compton are invited up to the girls' "pad" for some cheap thrills. One of the girls offers Joe some marijuana. Joe demurs. "You aren't chicken, are ya?" she teases. "No, I'm not chicken," and turning to Compton, he asks, "You aren't chicken are ya?" And they smoke and they "ball" and for a little while, they are content.

Overtaken by events which they can't possibly understand, they can only look to each other for some measure of reality. "You aren't chicken, are ya?" epitomises their disorientation. Lulled by the easy sex and addled by the billowing cloud of marijuana smoke, Joe and Bill look to each other for assurance that traditional values haven't disappeared from the face of the earth. They are searching for some sign that the chicken is still with them.

Sadly though, it is not. Bill pays for his earlier crime, for his hypocrisy and for his philandering by accidentally shooting his daughter in the back with a high-powered rifle. In this maelstrom, the chicken cannot come to rest.

See: *Rebel Without A Cause.*

KING KONG (1931)

As astringent a political allegory as *Gulliver's Travels* or *Alice in Wonderland*, the creators of this "horror picture" foresaw class war, *mano a mano*, waiting to erupt in the towns and cities of America. Just as it is Big Business against the Little Guy in the States, on Skull Island downtrodden chickens have no chance against a giant rampaging ape.

Kong pounds on the gates surrounding a native village, demanding his virgin sacrifice. The symbolism is inelegant but brutally accurate. Kong represents industry's "fat cats", heedless to the needs of those whom they employ. The natives symbolise middle-management. The chickens which both the ape and the natives recklessly trample to death are America's "forgotten men" and cast-off women, the old, the sick, the stupid, the worker, the artist.

Cameraman Edward Linden was directed (by Merian C. Cooper and by Ernest B. Schoedsack) to capture all the flurry and flight of the chickens as they fell beneath the feet of panic-stricken natives and their collapsing huts (American society). Hundreds of chickens are crushed amid the hysteria. Editor Ted Cheeseman cut this footage to only a few seconds of screen time, it is believed, on the "advice" of the Lobby, whose members feared that the "parody was directed at them."[22]

See: *Gone With the Wind.*

'King Kong': primitive chickens, modern issues.

KRAMER VS KRAMER (1979)

Curious circumstances surround Robert Benton's decision to soften his support of the chicken in American cinema. After directing truly ambitious scenes (*Bad Company*) and writing gracefully poetic scenes (*Bonnie and Clyde*), he returns with a film characterised by one of its stars as "a soap opera" and a chicken scene which rivals advertisements of toilet tissue for its evasiveness and timidity.

Struggling to fill the sexual and emotional void left by his wife's departure, Ted Kramer (Dustin Hoffman) takes his assistant, Phyllis (Jobeth Williams) home to bed. In the middle of the night Phyllis, as naked as the day she was born, makes her way to the bathroom. She runs into (almost *over*) Kramer's young son Billy (Justin Henry). All the boy can think to ask her is, "Do you like fried chicken?" All that Phyllis can think to answer as she backs away, mimicking the pose of the Botticelli *Venus*, is, "Yes...I...do."

Pivotally, the child's innocence brings him a clear understanding of the chicken's influence on everyday life. Phyllis's reaction typifies the embarrassing distance that modern, "sophisticated" adults keep between their lives and any awareness of that influence. The theme is an old Council chestnut. Despite that fact, the hit-and-miss wisdom of Academy members awarded the film a Best Picture Oscar.

See: *Rock 'n' Roll High School; Taxi Driver*.

LA DOLCE VITA (1961)

Traditional values (the nuclear family, romantic love, fair play, etc.) are cast off like old shoes for the sake of the "modern" and the "synthetic". Chickens and women are debased as society rips apart at the seams.

Newspaperman Marcello Rubino (Marcello Mastroianni) pursues the sensual Sylvia (Anita Ekberg), a Hollywood film star visiting Rome. Their appetite for an increasing volume and variety of sensual pleasure is senseless and sterile and climaxes in an orgy that is devoid of passion and of any real purpose.

Drunk and disorderly, Mercello rides on the back of a pliant woman, dowsing her with liquor, calling her his "chicken", and finally, breaking a pillow over her so that the chicken feathers which pour out of it stick to her flesh. She is a parody of a woman and a parody of a chicken. Marcello is a parody of a man.

"They have been driven from our consciousness," Page Smith writes of the 20th Century chicken, "by the terrible and irresistible logic of technology...Surely (these) creatures...will continue to exist under the auspices of our...society, but...*they will not be chickens and their eggs will not be eggs*." Federico Fellini made this same statement 15 years before those words were written.

See: Introduction, vi; *Professor, Beware*.

LACOMBE, LUCIEN (1974)

Director Louis Malle (LOO-ee MAHL) set out to render, compassionately, the horrible ambiguities of life in France during the German Occupation. Politics are distilled to personal experience.

Lucien Lacombe (the "Lacombe, Lucien" of the title) is played by Pierre Blaise, who died tragically in a road accident not long after the film was completed. Lacombe is a frustrated farm-boy anxious to command the respect of other villagers and the love of a beautiful girl. The Nazis offer him the opportunity to work as a collaborator. Lacombe, not one to look a gift Fascist in the mouth, accepts their offer.

In a sweeping tracking shot, Malle captures the intense Lacombe striding across the farmyard, carrying a live chicken by its feet. With a few masterful swipes, he slaps the chicken's head off.

The act is one of self-mutilation. The chicken embodies the personal tragedy of Lacombe's life, which is a social tragedy as well. After the war, the real Lacombe was executed by the Free French.

LAEMMLE, CARL

The founding father and guiding light of Universal Pictures, Laemmle built his studios on the property known as Taylor Ranch. The greater part of the ranch's income derived from its huge flock of chickens. Laemmle continued to raise chickens through the mid-thirties. If, as he feared, the motion picture business proved to be unprofitable, his chickens would continue to provide support for his family.

The first meeting of the Chicken Lobby (which evolved into the more imposing Council) was at Taylor Ranch. Petaluma was at that time (circa 1925) a distant El Dorado, a place which served primarily as an inspiration to the film community. While he lived, Laemmle and Taylor Ranch were a beacon to the first American film artists, entrepreneurs and chicken idealists from every walk of life. Carl Laemmle died in 1939.

Russ Meyer star, Stu Lancaster with Astrid de Wild.

LANCASTER, STUART

The actor who co-starred in a string of Russ Meyer's features is, in conversation, modest and thoughtful. "As an actor and as a person, I've always been challenged by the parts I do for Russ. It was Russ who taught me the truth about chickens. I didn't believe him at first, I thought, 'this is a joke'. I guess it was impossible to see the whole picture while I was in the middle of it."

It was when Lancaster saw the final cut of *Faster, Pussycat! Kill! Kill!* that he fully understood the scope of the work he had done. "We were in a screening room in Hollywood, and after the fried chicken scene I looked over at Russ and I saw he was looking at me. We just smiled at each other. We both knew."

It was a short step from eating fried chicken on camera to "making love" to a live chicken on camera, a simulated act Lancaster performed for his part in *Supervixens*. "It seemed like the only logical next step...it's not only my acting I want to perfect, if that's possible, I want to have some understanding of life. Now, to me that means getting as close to chickens as I can. There's so much that depends on it."

See: *Faster, Pussycat! Kill! Kill!;* Meyer, Russ; *Supervixens.*

LANDIS, JOHN

Our interview with John Landis began icily when we asked him directly whether he would acknowledge the existence and influence of the Council. His answer to us was as direct as our question. "I can't comment on that." Casual conversation and a small amount of flattery drew him out. When we asked him whether the chicken scene in *Animal House* was improvised or whether it appeared in the shooting script, his response sent a chill down our spines. "It was strongly suggested by corporate entities."

As the afternoon wore on, the legendary Landis reserve wore down and he admitted that he was hedging. "I hesitate to be entirely truthful. This information in the wrong hands could injure many people. There is a great deal of prejudice for and against chickens and knowledge, true knowledge, of chickens. Films are an *insignificant* part. You guys are being used."

Used by whom? Certainly not by Virgin Books, who paid us money to do this work. "Your publisher is being used," he flatly declared. A long minute of silence followed and then was shattered by Landis' whispered accusation: "By the Council"

We continued our conversation on the back lot of Universal Studios. Landis had not yet installed "anti-bugging" devices in his office. "Directors are directed by the Council, it's as simple as that. I'll give you an example. In the Country Bunker scene I wanted them to play behind glass. We arrived on the set and there was no glass — there was chickenwire. We had to use it, we had no choice."

His voice, confident, almost serene when we first met became hushed and unsteady. "I work in the shadow of the Black Tower*. People have been killed for bad-mouthing MCA."

But surely the promotion of chicken consciousness, the elevation of chicken consequence through feature films, is an objectively good thing. "You don't understand," Landis spat out, "You guys are being fooled. The Council is behind, underneath and on top of things you've got no idea about!" He started to rant. "The assassination of John Kennedy, the sinking of the Andrea Doria, UFO's, the cattle mutilations you've been hearing so much about, Judge Crater — Judge Crater was *on* to them! He was going to talk and then *bam*"!

We tried our best to calm him, to reassure him that others have spoken out. "Michael Ritchie. I'll tell you something about Michael Ritchie — tremendous ties with the oil companies, chicken farms in Mexico." Suddenly, the storm had passed. Landis stood quietly in front of the *Psycho* house. "It will be revealed soon. The truth, the rise of the Third World. People die because of it. I don't think you realise what you've uncovered."

When we returned with him to his office, Sean Daniel, who was then and is at this writing Vice President of Universal Pictures, was waiting for us. Landis turned pale and in mid-sentence substituted the word "spatula" for the word "chicken". Daniel shot Landis a steely glance and said dryly, "Don't you mean 'chicken', John?" Saying nothing more, he turned and walked out of the office.

Landis slumped into his desk chair. "The fear of death doesn't frighten me as much as ridicule."

See: *Animal House; Blues Brothers, The.*

LAWRENCE OF ARABIA (1963)

Political idealist or megalomaniac? Homosexual or sensualist? Sadist or masochist? Egoist or altruist? User or used? T.E. Lawrence was probably all of these things in different combinations at different times. Sometimes he was a sadistic, egoistical, homosexual megalomaniac and sometimes he was a masochistic, altruistic political idealist. David Lean attempted a portrait of the shadowy British soldier whose body and soul were maimed in his struggle to "give the Arabs their freedom".

As a director sensitive to the ability of *pictures* to convey a greater depth of meaning than words, Lean composed a chicken scene which offers the only insight we can have into Lawrence's character: that we

*Also called the Death Star, the skyscraper functions as the executive offices of Universal Pictures and West coast headquarters of UP's parent company, MCA.

John Landis in front of the 'Psycho' house at Universal.

MCA INC. 100 UNIVERSAL CITY PLAZA, UNIVERSAL CITY, CALIFORNIA 91608, 213-985-4321

Executive Offices

October 9, 1980

Jon-Stephen Fink
Mieke van der Linden
473 South Bedford Drive
Beverly Hills, Calif. 90210

Dear Jon and Mieke,

Enclosed are the only two stills I could put my hands on quickly of the infamous "four fried chickens and a coke" scene from "The Blues Brothers".

After carefully considering the information I related to you this afternoon, I feel it is my duty to warn you that your lives may be in danger. I strongly suggest staying away from any fast food franchises or Italian restaurants. You may have thought I was kidding when I brought up the cattle mutilations, the Kennedy assassinations, and the Judge Crater disappearance, but I assure you that something deep and sinister is indeed going on. Your harmless book on chickens in the cinema may become Pandora's Box.

Watch the skies!

Sincerely,

John Landis!

John Landis

Enc.

 can have no insight into Lawrence's character.

El Aurens, as Lawrence is called by the Arabs, has combined hostile Bedouin tribes into a single army which he will lead to attack the Turkish-held port city of Aqaba. We watch the battle procession from inside a tent. We do not see Lawrence, only the event that he has created — thousands of men and camels and horses parading to war. In a corner of the tent (in the lower right corner of the screen) the silhouette of a chicken appears for an instant, emerging then retreating into deeper shadows. Like the chicken, Lawrence's "whole" self cannot be known. Like all of our heroes, he appears before us at a providential moment, rewrites history and is gone, "like the shadow of an Arab chicken".[23]

LONGEST YARD, THE (1974)

Also released under the title *The Mean Machine*, Robert Aldrich directed this comedy-drama set in a Florida prison. Burt Reynolds is Paul Crewe, ex-pro football star, who captains a team of his fellow inmates against a team of prison guards.

During the first half of the game, inmate Richard Kiel ("Jaws" of the Bond thrillers) "closelines"* one of the guards. "I think I broke his fucking neck," he says. The guards' game becomes more cautious. The next words we hear are the radio announcer's (Michael Ford): "It's a kind of timid or chicken kind of football."

An American football, similar to a Rugby ball, is egg shaped. The ball is both a potential friend and a potential enemy to any player at a given time. In a sense, that quality is determined both by the strategy of the teams (which exist beyond and around an individual player) and the skill of the players themselves. Because the game in *The Longest Yard* is played between society (the guards) and the anti-social (the inmates), the "chicken kind of football" becomes a moral struggle. In the end, the inmates win.

MA AND PA KETTLE AT HOME (1954)

The popular characters first portrayed by Marjorie Main and Percy Kilbride in *The Egg and I* return in Charles Lamont's elegant rendering of American society threatened from within by the decline of traditional one-family farms. Ma and Pa have less than one week to turn their run-down farm into a model of modern agriculture so that their son Elwin (Brett Halsey) can win a scholarship to agricultural school.

Elwin's essay on the marvels of his parents' farm, all of them fabricated in the boy's imagination, wins him a place as a finalist in the contest for the scholarship. The first his father hears of it is when it is broadcast over the radio, which he listens to in the chicken coop. "I keep it for the

*A blocking technique frowned upon by football purists, it involves the use of the extended arm raised to the opponent's throat level. To be effective, the defensive arm must be very large.

Ma Kettle (Marjorie Main) explains the behaviour of an eccentric hen to Alphonsus Mannering (Alan Mobray).

hens," he says. Standing in the ramshackle coop he hears Elwin describe it as "a chicken-house made of glass bricks." This is a puzzle to Pa.

The Kettles are due to be visited by a contest judge who will decide whether Elwin's or his girlfriend Sally's (Alice Kelley) farm is the more modern. During a romantic interlude between the young lovers (accompanied by subtle undertones of chickens cackling), Sally's mean-tempered father (Irving Bacon) advises her to "clean out the chicken-house before dark." This was a favourite expression among Egyptian nobles during the reign of Akhenaton.

Chickens punctuate almost every scene of the film, a steady crescendo of incidents which climax in a bedroom at the Kettle's. The contest judge, Mannering (Alan Mobray) climbs wearily into bed. "Ah!" he exclaims. "There's a thing in there!" Ma Kettle, unruffled as ever, reaches between the sheets and pulls out her prize hen. "She will not nest with the other chickens in the chicken-house," Ma explains. Released into the rafters, the hen lays an egg on Mannering's forehead.

Lamont worked well within the Council's understood guidelines and composed a film that was coherent artistically as well as satisfying to the Council. He produced consistently bankable films which broadly assert acceptable and enduring truths about chickens and their relationship to human beings. Screenwriter Kay Lenard, described privately both as "a loyal functionary"[24] and a "lick-spittle lackey of the running dogs of chicken imperialism"[25], executed a script which made poetic use of rural imagery without pre-empting Lamont's perspective. "I keep the radio for the hens" is a line which is characteristic of Lenard's acute perception of the chicken's timeless consequence. Pa Kettle instinctively maintains continuity with Sumerian peasants and at the same time bows to the hens' spiritual ascendance — it is they who have use for the "airwaves" which are present but invisible.

The hen with Mannering exercises her freedom outside the boundary of the chicken house and lives in the human house, engendering happiness and prosperity (the egg).

See: Introduction, iv and v.

MALICK, TERENCE

The forceful director of *Badlands* and *Days of Heaven*, his chicken scenes are characterised by their poetic intensity. Malick is clearly an artist whose career has benefitted from hewing to the political line established by the younger members of the Council.

Like Robert Benton, those who decide such things are seeing that Malick has a lot to do and will probably reward his industriousness with an Oscar — either Best Picture or Best Director — within the next five years. His stationery does not bear an address or phone number, and a curious fact casts suspicion on the authorship of the letter we received. We consulted a telephone directory to find a listing for "Merrily Weiss". The directory, which was attached to a public phone near the Venice Division police station (the letter was postmarked Marina Del Rey, a wealthy community adjacent to Venice), was missing the page that would have included the name Weiss, Merrily.

TERRY MALICK

August 25, 1980

Jon-Stephen Fink
Mieke van der Linden
473 S. Bedford Drive
Beverly Hills, CA
90210

Dear Mr. Fink and Ms. van der Linden,

Terry Malick is out of the country and has asked me to answer his mail in his absence. Unfortunately, our schedule becomes more frantic and unpredictable everyday and does not allow me to promise any of Mr. Malick's vastly overbooked time. I wish you luck with your publication.

Sincerely,

Merrily Weiss

Merrily Weiss
Assistant to
Terry Malick

A close inspection of the typeface of Malick's stationery and that of Ellen Burstyn reveals a stunning similarity.

See: *Badlands*; Burstyn, Ellen; *Days of Heaven*.

MARRY ME, (1925)

James Cruze, a founding member of the Chicken Lobby, directed this adaptation of the play "The Nest Egg" by Anne Caldwell. In it, Hetty Gandy (Florence Vidor), an attractive school teacher, visits a chicken farm and falls in love with John Smith (John Roche) who proposes marriage.

Before Hetty can come to a decision she is called away, leaving behind an egg inscribed with the date on which she will marry the love-struck chicken farmer. The egg is supposed to be served to John for breakfast but goes by mistake into cold storage.

Five years later, through an improbable series of unlucky circumstances, Hetty is forced to spend the night in a hotel with another man called John Smith (Edward Everett Horton). To shield Hetty from scandal, Smith marries her. They grow to love each other and Hetty's love cures him of his hypochondria.

It had been only four years since the Nelson debacle and the film industry was quick to alter its course. The advertisements never mention the plot's mainspring — the inscribed egg, and the meeting of Hetty and John Smith No. 1 on a chicken farm, a fact which draws chickens together with human romance and sexuality, is merely glossed over. *Marry Me* was an extreme reaction to the reception of *Chickens* and began a conservative trend which continued for several years.

See: *Rainmaker, The*.

MAZURSKY, PAUL

"Take the 'k' out of 'chicken' and you've got a stupid word — chicen. It means nothing."

Paul Mazursky is forthright about the responsibility shared by film-makers to keep the chicken in the popular consciousness. "It's a very normal thing, like bringing flowers to somebody in the hospital."

One of Mazursky's dreams is to direct a film which makes a significant chicken statement, and he has a story in mind. "It would be about a chicken who looks like a man and I'd set it in Germany after the war."

Having enjoyed a position in the mainstream of the film industry for many years, he is acutely aware that studios today are terrified "of laying an egg." He told us that despite recent successes like *Star Wars* (no chicken scene) and *Jaws* (no chicken scene), it is a "very nervous time for the industry."

Mazursky expressed his appreciation for the opportunity to be counted among those people dedicated to raising chicken consciousness "the

Paul Mazursky, chicken auteur.

world over" by confessing, "It's a rare thing for somebody to tell me they want ten minutes with me and they actually stay ten minutes and don't ask me for a job."

See: Delmarva Poultry Festival, *The; Next Stop, Greenwich Village; Sunshine Boys, The.*

MEYER, RUSS

In his "eagle's nest" high in the Hollywood Hills, Russ Meyer spoke about fried chicken, live chickens and his most famous chicken scene, featuring Stuart Lancaster in *Supervixens*.

"No, Stu was happy to do it. I explained the artistic necessity and he understood right away." The actor and the director, agreeing that a hen was the physical and aesthetic compliment to a corn cob, worked out the complicated logistics of shooting Lancaster while he ran, naked, clutching a chicken to his loins. "Stu didn't seem to mind the number of takes we shot, not at all."

Even though the sex between Lancaster and the hen was simulated, it aroused the private envy of established directors. "Oh, I'd get phone calls from people saying they were Peter Bogdanovich or Paul Mazursky or somebody, Howard Zieff, and they'd tell me how much they admired the fact that I could write, shoot and release any chicken scene I wanted to, it's all my decision."

On the subject of his prerogative, why *did* he decide on such a scene? "We chose that on the basis of the Kinsey Report. The chicken is the animal most used for sex on the farm. You'd think that the hole is too small, but look — it's big enough for an egg to come out of."

As an independent who once shot industrial films, Meyer's use of chicken imagery is instinctive and fundamental. The imaginative use of fried chicken in *Faster, Pussycat! Kill! Kill!* is a modern rendering of the more studied scene in *Tom Jones*. "Fried chicken is perfect for the family to be eating — it's cheap and suggestive and it ties the Old Man and his sons to the kid who was murdered. Varla calls him 'chicken' before the race, remember."

Meyer works virtually alone, producing, shooting, directing and editing and he scoffs at the existence of any "governing body" which instructs film-makers to include or exclude chickens from their work. He has passed through Petaluma many times but has never noticed anything "out of the ordinary" there.

See: *Faster, Pussycat! Kill! Kill!;* Lancaster, Stuart; *Supervixens.*

Russ Meyer demonstrates a subtle grasp of chicken consciousness.

MIDNIGHT EXPRESS (1979)

The bizarre tale of Billy Hayes, convicted of attempting to smuggle hashish out of Turkey, pivots around the nature of the mystical bond between chickens and fugitives.

Hayes (Brad Davis) is given a "break" of sorts after his arrest. He volunteers to lead Turkish officials to the taxi driver who sold him the 2 kilos of hashish. Hayes makes a mad dash for freedom.

He runs into a poultry shop and hides behind the crates and cages of chickens. As he presses his face close to one cage, the chickens, alarmed, begins to cackle wildly. This show of kinship for Hayes, unfortunately, panics him and alerts his pursuers. On his way out, to certain capture, he trips over another cage.

Inadvertently, the chickens become agents of the oppressors, their motives misunderstood by a boy in search of an "altered state of consciousness". The caged chickens forecast Hayes' fate and become linked at least in their distress.

The point that during times of crisis and hysteria chickens acquire *personal* symbolism is rarely (or so succinctly) made.

See: Parker, Alan.

Billy Hays (Brad Davis) comes face to face with his fate in a poultry warehouse.

MYSTERIOUS ISLAND (1961)

As a handful of lucky men escape in an observation balloon from the horrors of life in a Rebel prison during the Civil War, a grave voice intones, "This was just the beginning. We were prisoners of the wind."

Fate deals the fugitives a winning hand. A storm carries them to a mysterious island somewhere in the South Pacific. The island's bounty and its perils reveal themselves all at once in the form of giant wildlife — giant oysters, giant crabs, giant bees and at least one giant prehistoric chicken.

Special effects master Ray Harryhausen created the mutant "chick" which attacks war correspondent Spillett (Gary Merrill) and which is killed, apparently, by young buck Herbert Brown (Michael Callan),

Prehistoric chicken? Even the "experts" are baffled.

plunging a knife remorselessly into the bird's throat.

When the company, which by this time has added two shipwrecked women to its number, feast on the bird, Neb (Dan Jackson), the cheerful, picturesque Negro jokes, "If it wasn't for you, Herbert, Mr. Spillett would've been on the inside cutting out instead of the outside cutting in!"

Even though *Mysterious Island* is discounted as a bantam-weight fantasy, Cy Enfield directed it as classical drama. The nuances and subtle allusions to primitive ritual put it in a class by itself. The basic appetite (hunger) is the reason why, on this remote island, chicken and human become one. The chicken becomes human when a human eats chicken flesh, and likewise, the humans have strength in their bodies now, the virtue of the chicken.

Sadly, the "prehistoric" chicken is the result of careless genetic tampering and the island, as if in revolt against the pretentious, puny hand of man, explodes and sinks into the sea.

See: *Food of the Gods; Sleeper.*

NASHVILLE (1975)

In what is generally acknowledged to be Robert Altman's last significant film, chickens hover on the fringes of the social fabric as it rips apart. Barbara-Jean (Ronee Blakely) is an emotionally unstable Country Western singer. On her return to Nashville she is signed, by her manager-husband, to perform in a show at a theme park. Barbara-Jean isn't ready to do anything in front of anyone.

During her act she suffers an emotional breakdown. She drifts into and out of her song, idly chatting about Tennessee, her house and finally, her childhood. Just before she leaves the stage (and sensible reality) she performs an impersonation of her grandfather's impersonation of chickens. It is very good.

To survive the tensions straining her, Barbara-Jean can only move *backward*, to childhood, for safety and security. In a social sense, Altman (and Blakely — it was she who invented her chicken scene) suggests that we need to move backward in order to move forward. A second chicken scene substantiates this idea.

Barbara-Jean lies in her hospital bed. Next to her is her husband Ashley (Allan Garfield, now Goorwitz). Next to Ashley are cartons of Kentucky Fried Chicken. In this context the fried chicken is the link between where Barbara-Jean "is" and where she "has gone". She has gone backward in her own life and forward in the life of the race.

This concept is neatly spelled out in Ferenczi's so-called *thalassal regressive trend*. An imaginative psychoanalyst, he proposed that there was a time in the chicken's biological past when it evolved from a "fish" into a "bird". When chickens were "fish" they reproduced the way present-day fish reproduce. The female deposits her eggs and the male releases his sperm over them. The sperm is kept alive by the salt water. Ferenczi tells us that these "sea chickens" were driven from the sea by some nameless horror and when they tried to reproduce on land the way they reproduced in the water, most of them died ugly deaths. The few who didn't die evolved wombs, miniature oceans inside them, and produced eggs with shells. Sex and madness, according to Ferenczi, are the only means we have of journeying back to the safety of those primordial seas.

Barbara-Jean had already begun that journey. It is the destination of our race and so, of society. Like Barbara-Jean, human society has limits to the amount of stress it can tolerate. Through "madness", individuals in a society pull it "backward" (forward) against its will. The stress becomes too great and society itself breaks down. Altman dramatises this collapse with Barbara-Jean's violent death, her chickens stilled forever.

See: *Network*; Tewkesbury, Joan.

Barbara-Jean (Ronee Blakley) suffers complete personality disintegration onstage in Nashville. Blakley devised the chicken scene herself.

NETWORK (1976)

In his Academy Award-winning screenplay, Paddy Chayevsky exposed the ghouls who own and operate America's television industry. He also achieved a subtle statement concerning the place of chickens in the news media.

A gang of terrorists is holed up in a large frame house. A pick-up truck pulls up in front and, as it stops, a small flock of chickens dashes in front of it. Inside the house with the terrorists and with an aggressive T.V. executive (Faye Dunaway), half-empty (half-full) boxes of Kentucky Fried chicken are placed randomly around the kitchen.

The progression from live chickens to fried chickens is a variation on the same theme used one year before in Robert Altman's *Nashville.* Sidney Lumet though, intends his images to make explicit the process of packaging. Just as the chickens are seen first in their natural state, then "after processing", so the terrorists become a pre-packaged "media event".

The question in the corridors of the Writers Guild after the 1976 Academy Award ceremony was, "Who 'packaged' *Network*?"

See: *Nashville*.

NEXT STOP, GREENWICH VILLAGE (1976)

Paul Mazursky is a film-maker who recognises that the chicken for the Jews is an important symbolic bird. Unable to resist the temptation, his sentimental return to the time and place of his youth includes a classic "Jewish mother with chicken product" scene. A cliché becomes a cliché by being consistently true.

Larry Lapinsky (Lenny Barker) has just moved into his own apartment. To be sure that her son is "eating all right", Mrs. Lapinsky (Shelley Winters) travels across town and delivers a boiled chicken.

The second day prior to Yom Kippur, a Jewish holiday, is the day of the *kapparah*, or the atonement. Men use cocks and the women use hens: "The homes are usually noisy. The fowls, their legs tied, cluck and crow at the tops of their voices. It generally happens, too, that a rooster gets excited and begins to run and fly all over the house, despite its bound feet, and there follows a long struggle to subdue him...

"First the fowl...is held in the hand and everyone reads selections from certain Psalms...Then the fowl is circled about the head nine times, the following being recited at the same time: 'This is instead of me, this is an offering on my account, this is in expiation for me; this rooster (or hen) shall go to his (or her) death...and I may enter a long and healthy life.' This rite is followed by the slaughter of the chickens..."[26]

That roughly describes what it is like for struggling young artists in a Jewish family. Larry succeeds in throwing off the humiliation and degradation which naturally attends such a life, strikes out on his own and "makes it" by landing a small part in a film about juvenile delinquents. In real life, Mazursky played a small role in *The Blackboard Jungle*.

See: *Goin' South*; Mazursky, Paul.

NICHOLSON, JACK

Despite three letters and over one hundred phone calls, Jack Nicholson was successful in eluding us. His unresponsiveness was a surprise and a bit of a shock. As a director, writer and actor he has done more to further the cause of chicken consciousness than anyone presently active in the film industry. His courage and insight evoke the spirit of the pioneering Jack Nelson, whose initials he shares.

Nicholson has been responsible for chicken scenes of tremendous depth (*Five Easy Pieces*), tenderness (*Goin' South*), wit (*Goin' South* and *The Fortune*), irony (*Chinatown*), imagination (*The Passenger*) and conscience (*Ride in the Whirlwind*). His exact relationship with the Council is unknown, even by those people who are close to him. Either Nicholson has a genius for becoming involved with material inherently chicken-conscious or these "plum" projects are intentionally steered his way. What the evidence suggests is that his attitude and ambition are genuine, having been established in the days before the Council had become the power-mongering dinosaur it now is.

See: *Five Easy Pieces; Goin' South;* Hellman, Monte.

Jack Nicholson has appeared in more chicken scenes than any other actor in the world. He is pictured here with Angelica Huston, daughter of director John Huston, with whom Nicholson shared the chicken scene in 'Chinatown'.

NIGHTMARE ALLEY (1947)

Tyrone Power as Stan Carlisle rises from obscurity to fame only to sink into ignominy as the "shrewd, selfish rascal" clawing his way to the top of the "spook racket". In his 28th film role, Power plays a charlatan mentalist, bilking rich people out of thousands of dollars. In the words of one *New York Times* reviewer, "...it would seem that a terrible retribution is the inevitable consequence for he who would mockingly attempt to play God."

Retribution comes at last as the wreckage of Carlisle's reckless deceits trips him up and he is made an outcast of outcasts. Carlisle's tale ends when he becomes a carnival geek, earning his living by biting the heads off live chickens. His fate echoes that of Cleopatra in *Freaks*, living life at the crudest level of chicken consciousness. Carlisle's closing line is his one genuine insight. The geek job is described to him and the boss asks him, "Think you can do it?" Carlisle sees the truth immediately, "Mister, I was made for it."

This is a morality play, no mistake, and one which bears the benchmark of the Lobby. In the early years of the Cold War founding members of that body were dying and being replaced by doctrinaire conservatives who established the Council. Carlisle's "spiel" was written at one of the first Council meetings, in Petaluma:

> Since the dawn of history, mankind has sought to see behind the veil which hides him from tomorrow. And through the ages certain men have gazed into the polished crystal and seen. Is it some property of the crystal itself? Or does the gazer use it to turn his gaze inward?

Power renamed the DC-3 owned by the studio and used to send him off on publicity trips,"The Geek".

See: *Freaks*.

NOSFERATU (1979)

Like the death of Christ, the death of Dracula, his sinister counterpart, is heralded by the crowing of a cock. Unlike Christ, in order for death to overtake him, Dracula must be detained by a woman "pure of heart" and then "the light of day will destroy him".

In Werner Herzog's retelling of the vampire legend, Dracula (Klaus Kinski), starved of love for centuries, allows a woman, Lucy Harker (Isabelle Adjani) to "detain" him "past the crow of the cock" and so, he is destroyed.

The rooster of death appears much earlier in the story, as the centrepiece of a cold buffet prepared by the count for his guest, Jonathan Harker (Bruno Ganz). Lucy's husband, Jonathan finds the laden table on arising after his first night in Dracula's castle, and his attention is drawn

A reverse of fortunes for Stan Carlisle (Tyrone Power, far right) leaves him with limited career opportunities in 'Nightmare Alley'. Joan Blondell (second from left) looks on.

immediately to the black rooster. He lifts the right wing gingerly and takes something — a nut? a grape? — from it, popping the morsel into his mouth. It is an unholy transubstantiation and Harker now is no longer Dracula's "guest", but his victim and heir.

The black rooster also awakes us to Herzog's symbolic use of colour — blue, black, red and white — throughout the film. Specifically, the bird's black feathers, suggesting mystery and death, and red wattle, suggesting blood and life, combine to foreshadow the fates of Lucy and Jonathan. For them, death is the death that romance brings — one death and one eternal, miserable life.

See: *Stroszek*

O'BANNON, DAN

"The most appealing quality of chickens is that they're naïve. You feel sorry when you eat them. And the way they flap their feathers, they're so ineffectual."

A curiously earthy view of chickens from the writer (*Alien; Dark Star*) who has done more to project chickens onto a cosmic backdrop than any other in the entire history of theatrical films. O'Bannon's early interest in

Dan O'Bannon writer of 'Dark Star' and 'Alien'.

chickens and in film emerged while he was in college in Missouri. His first film, made under the asupices of the Film Production Club was a 16mm speculative thriller called *Attack of the 50 Foot Chicken*. Its subject is "The disastrous results of an atomic mutation; nature runs wild as a chicken assumes enormous proportions and threatens to wipe out all life on earth."

It was a bold move for a young film-maker working on a shoestring in the cloistered backwaters of Missouri. O'Bannon recalled the technical difficulties associated with casting temperamental chickens in pivotal roles.

"All it had to do was walk across the table behind the planetarium. The camera started rolling, I released the chicken and it just stood there. I tried pushing it with a stick, I tried taping its feet to a piece of cardboard and moving it myself, I tried pulling it with a piece of rope. It all looked terrible. Then I had an idea. I gave it 15 milligrams of Dexedrine.

"After about five minutes the chicken was running from wall to wall and shitting all over the place. I caught it and held it still while my partner got behind the camera. I let the chicken go and it took off like a shot out of a gun. After about 15 minutes the Dexedrine wore off and the chicken fell into a deep depression, so we had to wrap for the day. It took us several days to get all the scenes, since the chicken was only good for

15 minutes a day."[27]

While we were discussing the chicken scene in *Dark Star* ("Chickens strike me as ludicrous. Whenever I want to show something ridiculous I bring in a chicken...") O'Bannon brought up the chicken scene in *Alien*. Although we had seen the picture, and while we enjoyed the part when the creature bursts out of John Hurt's chest, we could not remember any chicken anywhere in the story. "You wouldn't know it unless somebody pointed it out. When Ashe is looking at the X-Rays of Kane you see an embryo — big eyes, little beak...Ridley Scott found it in a 16mm educational film. It's a chicken embryo."

O'Bannon has a special admiration for the chicken art of Tobe Hooper, whose *Texas Chainsaw Massacre* contains powerful chicken footage. "In that living-room, all kinds of things are strewn around, and there are chickens in birdcages. It's a work of art by a deranged mentality — the world taken apart and put back together in a different way."

That idea extends to his concept of history. "There's no proof that dinosaurs didn't have feathers. They found fossilised skin from a duck-billed dinosaur and it wasn't smooth like a lizard's skin, it was knobbly. It's a possibility that the *tyrannosaurus rex* had a wattle and comb — maybe they just shrank."

See: *Dark Star*.

Alan Parker, Albert Finney and chicken on the set of 'Shoot the Moon'.

PARKER, ALAN

Taking his place in the vanguard of artists committed to "total disclosure", Alan Parker was the first of the directors we approached who acted on his pledge to "go public". In his first letter to us (June 5, 1980) he warned us that "tracking (the stills) down can be quite difficult..." Even for a man of Parker's standing in the film community the Council can make access to chicken footage subject to voluminous paperwork and even videotaped polygraph tests. Handing us the necessary disclaimer, Parker "admits" his feelings about chickens — he doesn't really "like them an awful lot", that he "directs them from a safe distance behind the camera car." He knows better than we what kind of "line" the Council censors will swallow.

In his second letter to us (July 21, 1980) signed with an even firmer hand, he enclosed the promised stills from *Bugsy Malone* and *Midnight Express*. Cautiously he characterises our investigation a "dedication to eccentricity". His support makes possible a time when those who have not yet come out of the shadows may speak the truth without being forced to camouflage their intention.

See: *Bugsy Malone; Midnight Express*.

PAT GARRETT AND BILLY THE KID (1973)

Mindless, unprovoked, pathological violence is impossible to explain in rational terms. The only thing that artists and chickens can do is to measure it and let society run its course.

When we first meet Billy the Kid (Kris Kristofferson), he and his friends are enjoying a little target practice. The targets are live chickens, immobilised by being half-buried in the ground. Close-ups of chicken bodies, chicken *lives* being blown to a pulp are the horrifying, unredeemable consequence of human depravity.

Sam Peckinpah is careful to direct our attention to the physical fact of the abuse before he hints at its deeper meaning. Helpless (abandoned) chickens, dying not so that hungry humans can eat, but heartlessly shotgunned into inert mush *for the goddamned hell of it* has to be an act beyond any sane person's ability to comprehend. This is Peckinpah's valuable contribution, arousing dormant compassion for individual chickens.

Does the "target practice" have any virtue at all? Only one. For one brief moment, the time it takes to aim a shotgun, one man and one chicken have between them what the philosopher Soren Kierkegaard describes as "a definitive relationship". Yet in the next moment, it is a thing of the past. The only solace which Peckinpah allows us is the solace we can take from the Kid's eventual murder at the hands of his onetime friend. As we live with chickens, so shall we die, as Dr. Dexter has often said.

The Pathé News "crowing rooster" trademark is the oldest in the industry. It stands as a symbol of unswerving dedication to the ideal of chicken awareness, which, through the famous "News Magazine of the Screen" series, was spread throughout the known world. The rooster was chosen by Charles Pathé in 1895 as "it was known since the time of the Gauls as an emblem of victory." The choice was prophetic.

Pathé was acquired by Warner Brothers Pictures, Inc. in 1947, where 38 theatrical short subjects and 81 editions of the News Magazine were

A revealing caricature of the Pathé brothers, Emil (left) and Charles (right).

produced. In 1956 Pathé News was sold to Pathé Pictures.

For those nine years, from 1947 to 1956, the theatrical newsreels — all heralded by the crowing rooster — were used by the Council as a primary indoctrination tool. Hundreds of directors, writers, producers, agents, will testify to having seen dozens of these films in their neighbourhood cinemas. The Council presidency was held by Jack L. Warner three times between 1947 and 1954: during the first quarter of 1947, the third and fourth quarters of 1950 and the fourth quarter of 1954. The times correspond roughly to the first stages of escalation in the Cold War, the Korean War and the winding down of the HUAC investigations — all events chronicled by Pathé News teams.

The Pathé archives are extensive, close to 30 million feet of film. Contained in them is nothing less than a visual and aural history of the 20th Century.

PATTON (1970)

Of the many chicken scenes which were prominent features of the script's final draft only a fragment of one of them appears in the film. Francis Coppola's screenplay and the film from it directed by Franklin J. Schaffner are as different from each other as feast from famine. In the opening minutes of the film a promise is made which is never kept.

A voice offscreen commands, "At-ten-shun!" We wait tensely for the first chickens to appear. But it is General George Patton (George C. Scott) whom we see first. "This individuality stuff is a lot of crap...We're going to murder those lousy Hun bastards by the bushel. Many of you boys are wondering whether you'll chicken out under fire. Don't worry about it..." It isn't until we arrive in the desert "near Kasserine" that we see chickens, and those are only indirectly associated with Patton. As the jeep carrying Omar Bradley (Karl Malden) screeches to a stop outside his headquarters, chickens scatter in front of it. In his script, Coppola dramatised Patton's first chicken encounter.

> 36 CLOSE SHOT — PATTON
> Eyes flashing, rage barely under control, he draws himself up and snaps off an ultrasmart salute to the ragged crew. Turning on his heel, he passes a crudely built sign designating II Corps Headquarters, on which a chicken squats. Nearby

> an Arab peddler leans, unimpressed, against a pen of chickens.

No such chicken scene appears in the film.

In April of 1969, the Council met in Petaluma to discuss the films to be released the following year. This is a fact, a matter of record. The documentation is in our possession.

One night during dinner, our doorbell rang. By the time I got to the door whomever had rung the bell had gone, but stuffed through the mail-slot in our front door was a wad of decorative paper, the kind used to wrap expensive gifts. Inside was a tape cassette and a coffee-stained carbon copy of what seemed to be a transcript. We played the tape, which was of poor quality, and found the place where the transcript began. The things we heard and the things we read startled us.

The conversation is between "Red Rooster", an alias disguising the identity, probably, of Fred Roos, at this writing a production head at Coppola's Zoetrope studios, and Franklin J. Schaffner. They are discussing the "treatment" for *Patton*, which Schaffner had routinely submitted.

RED ROOSTER: Where's the chickens, Frank?

SCHAFFNER: At the, in the tent, aren't they? When the kid, when Patton smacks the kid.

RED ROOSTER: There's no chickens in the tent. You mean he calls the kid 'chicken'?

SCHAFFNER: Well, he doesn't exactly use the word. You mean does he say 'chicken'? He calls him a coward. I have to work that out with Francis.*

RED ROOSTER: Do that. Work it out with Francis or whoever the hell you have to and let me have film, let's see — six weeks?

SCHAFFNER: You got it.

Only after a veiled threat that financing for the project would be withheld unless chickens were clearly shown to be a determining factor in the development of Patton's character, did Schaffner agree to specific revisions (see above). Given these circumstances, it is difficult to explain the absence of chickens in the version of the film that was finally released. A simple explanation may lie in the fact that power in the film industry shifts as quickly and mysteriously as the sands of the Sahara. While poetic, that reasoning is an oversimplification at odds with the

* Francis Ford Coppola

known facts about the Council's purpose and method. The truth about this film may never become known.

PEPE 1 AND PEPE 2

The twin roosters (Pepe 1 and Pepe 2) rose to stardom on the strength of the masterful efforts of their trainer and manager, Bob Anderson. Their featured role in *Roots*, the saga of Blacks in America, came about by "chance". "I just happened to mention the fighting roosters, three wild ones living on the ranch. The production manager at Warner's needed roosters."

In three short weeks, Anderson encouraged Pepe 1 and Pepe 2 to follow Chicken George (Ben Vereen) wherever he went and to crow on cue, a feat suggesting a greater degree of human-chicken communication than anyone connected with the production thought possible.

Bob Anderson has been a wrangler for too long a time to be convinced that anything involving chickens is "impossible". He has enjoyed the companionship of chickens and roosters for as long as he can remember. He worked with them on the two films which he regards as the only "true Westerns of the true West" — *Paint Your Wagon* and *How the West Was Won*.

Continuing their artistic partnership, Pepe 1, Pepe 2 and Anderson combined their talents to offer Marty Feldman an example of chicken élan for his comedy *In God We Trust*. Lying on their sides, each Pepe, on Anderson's cue, stood up, shook his feathers, leaped onto a perch and crowed into a megaphone. The relationship between Anderson and the two roosters is looked upon with a mixture of awe and envy by those fortunate enough to see them together at their ranch.

PLUCKED (1968)

The impressionistic opening credits roll over microphotographs of a developing chicken embryo. Virtually all of the story's style and substance is contained in this sequence.

Jean-Louis Trintignant, Ewe Aulin and Gina Lollobrigida are the leading players in this dramatic study of the kinds of passions which can be excited on an ultra-modern chicken farm in Northern Italy. The first scene is faintly evocative of Antonioni's *Blow-up*. In a rhythmic montage, Marco (Trintignant), his wife Anna (Lollobrigida) and their "guest" Gabriella (Aulin) take pictures of each other at play in the huge chicken-house. They hold fluffy white chickens and they pose beside a chute which is disgorging plucked chicken carcasses; they laugh and joke, childlike in their innocence. Watching them from outside are the impoverished workers whose jobs were taken away by automation. They stand there silently until Anna orders them away. "What did they want?" Gabriella asks. Anna answers her. "They wanted to kill us, that

Bob Anderson, chicken wrangler with Pepe 1 or Pepe 2?

should be obvious."

The second thing that is obvious is that Anna is a spiteful, embittered woman with lesbian tendencies. Marco's pursuit of the tantalising Gabriella is obvious too, and odious to his wife from the start. Accepting the risk, Marco presses on, as he explains to Gabriella how things are between him and Anna. "I was doing experiments in poultry breeding and she owned the largest poultry farm in Italy...But I began to long for my own identity, someone I could shelter and protect."

Later, on a midnight prowl to find Gabriella, Marco wanders into the chickenhouse. We see, in extreme close-up, chickens poking their heads out of their cages, mimicking and mocking Marco's desire. Gabriella's voice floats up from behind the cages.

Two themes develop side by side — the romantic triangle of Marco, Anna and Gabriella and the political intrigue of a poultry advisory board known as the Association. It is a blatant imitation of the Council. The conference room of its office suite is decorated with an enormous egg sculpture and a chicken portrait done in the style of Picasso's Blue Period. Marco, on Anna's behalf, attends a meeting the purpose of which is to contrive a strategy to promote poultry to "gourmets and connoisseurs."

Is the Association progressive or regressive, beneficial or detrimental? It is neither; the Association *is*. Borrowing a page from Karl Marx's famous book, the Association is the intermediate stage in the advance of worldwide chicken consciousness. We are left with the feeling that there will come a time when no association or council will need to exist — chickens will emerge to promote themselves. In *Plucked* the chickens endure when humans and their schemes destroy themselves.

See: *Fox, The.*

Gina Lollobrigida groomed from the beginning for her leading role in 'Plucked'.

Turkey or chicken? Charles Laughton nibbles a drumstick in 'The Private Life of Henry VIII'. Expert photo analysis reveals unmistakably chicken-like "toes". Spokesmen for the Korda family deny that chickens were anywhere on the set during shooting.

PRIVATE LIFE OF HENRY VIII, THE (1933)

Alexander Korda directed Charles Laughton as the monarch desperately searching for the "right woman" in the production hailed by critics as "the best picture to come out of a British studio."

Henry's vulgarity at table was a selling point for the film in America. According to independent observers*, the bird which is the source of the drumstick is a turkey, not a chicken. We prefer to trust the evidence of a memo dated October 25, 1932. It is from Alexander Korda to Victor Korda, the production designer.

> ...and be sure it is a *big* chicken with the foot still on.

The Kordas were determined to make one point about royalty in general and King Henry VIII in particular: it is the responsibility of the privileged to set the moral tone of society. In a line of succession, Henry's relationship to chickens is crude (the chicken foot) but engenders the possibility of refinement (his velvet cap). Eventually, chickens will be recognised as humanity's "legitimate heirs".

The love theme, "What Shall I Do For Love" by King Henry VIII was sung by Binnie Barnes.

*John Landis

Chicken in the hand, but the mystery grows deeper still. Genevieve Page and Robert Stephens in 'The Private Life of Sherlock Holmes.'

PRIVATE LIFE OF SHERLOCK HOLMES, THE (1970)

For many years Billy Wilder has made films which reflect the dominant mood in Petaluma. During the more aggressive of the late Fifties, he scored with *Some Like It Hot*. In the cooler early Seventies he responded with a chicken scene which for its restraint, is substantial and finely crafted.

While his use of chickens rarely amplifies the theme or plot, Wilder never fails to remind us that chickens have always been a significant feature of human life. Here, Sherlock Holmes (Robert Stephens) and Gabrielle Valladon (Genevieve Page) enjoy a Platonic love affair during his investigation of her husband's disappearance. The picnic is a romantic interlude which brings the two closer together (each eats a chicken leg), though their love will never be consummated (where is the *rest* of the chicken?).

According to one review, "the subject of the film is sex."

See: *Some Like It Hot*.

PROFESSOR, BEWARE (1938)

As an Egyptologist on everybody's Ten Most Wanted list, Harold Lloyd is forced by circumstance to hide a live chicken under his coat. This he must do to secure a car ride from a total stranger. When the chicken tries to announce itself by clucking, Lloyd pretends (with some success) that he is practising his chicken impersonation, which the stranger dismisses as second rate. When a car passes them in the opposite direction, honking its horn, the stranger applauds the faithfulness of that chicken noise.

This is a later Lloyd, less audacious than the Lloyd we remember from *Safety Last*, for instance, but it is also a much more reflective piece of work. As an archaeologist, Lloyd is the bridge which spans millennia, making possible a "dialogue" between the chickens of ancient Egypt and the chickens of today (the car horn).

The shadowy figure of the stranger introduces a consistent theme of films made between the wars — the distance that the modern mechanized world creates between the lives of chickens and the lives of people. It is, after all, the car horn to which he responds, not the living chicken.

See: *La Dolce Vita.*

PROPHECY (1979)

This is a valuable film for many reasons, not least of which is that the first chicken scene occurs within ten minutes of the opening credits.

Crusading public health doctor Rob Vern (Robert Foxworth) arrives at a tenement in the heart of Washington, D.C. He is led upstairs ("Right up there, sir...") and into a room where he finds a baby screaming in pain. The infant's mother cries with tears of frustration and rage. The mother, who bears a strange resemblence to Hattie MacDonald, complains to Dr. Vern that she has already been visited by another doctor. "He said this is chicken pox. I said to him they ain't no chickens in here, they rats in here." Her irony, sarcasm and scorn are not wasted on Dr. Vern who fearlessly diagnoses the baby's complaint as "rat bites".

Sent then to Maine to make an environmental impact study, Dr. Vern and his wife Maggie (Talia Shire) have to contend with her pregnancy, a rampaging raccoon, a killer salmon, a gargantuan tadpole and a psychopathic mutant bear. Dr. Vern discovers that as a result of the poisonous waste produced by a paper mill, the ecosystem is in mad revolt. Significantly, chickens never appear as "freaks" or mutants, they merely disappear. We see them once, at an Indian "village", where Dr. Vern has come to take blood samples, and never see them again.

Comparable to *Dr. Strangelove* as a glum view of our prospects for survival, *Prophecy* drives home one clear message — if we are truly bent on self-destruction, chickens will not stay to watch us die. In Richard Elfman's *Forbidden Zone*, a "cult" film first seen at Filmex (the annual Los Angeles film festival) an appeal is made for guidance from the chicken world. Squeezit Henderson speaks to the chickens:

CHICKEN: You know that chickens are always ready to help.

17 SQUEEZIT: But what can chickens do?
CHICKEN: Precisely.

This represents a radical change of direction for director John Frankenheimer, who in 1962 directed the uplifting *Birdman of Alcatraz*.

See: *Food of the Gods*.

RAINMAKER, THE (1957)

The neo-biblical psalm of drought and fertility, literal and figurative, real and imagined, in the land and in a woman marked an important step forward in the art of chickens in film. The script by N. Richard Nash was brought to life by the performances of Katharine Hepburn and Burt Lancaster, who together lent the chicken a "high brow" appeal it had only sporadically enjoyed.

Hepburn plays the scrappy, self-reliant Lizzie Curry opposite Lancaster's poetic, romantic rainmaker, Starbuck. In his first sales pitch Starbuck describes the way the sky looked the moment before he last drew rain from it. "There was a cloud the size of a mare's tail and another cloud like a white-washed chickenhouse..."

Nash's vision of Lizzie's spinsterhood, her "dry season" and the surrounding physical drought is echoed in the Curry barnyard — not one chicken is anywhere to be seen. Starbuck's chickenhouse in the sky is his promise of fertility.

"Take a chance on a con man," Starbuck challenges, "You gotta take my deal because a hundred bucks is a hundred bucks but rain in a dry season is beautiful to behold." Rain comes and so, later we assume, chickens return to the Curry farm.

Suggestions that Lizzie and the farm are metaphors for the world and that Starbuck and the rain are metaphors for chickens and redemption have been put forward by scholars but ideas like these only result from the strain of having to read dissertations for degrees in American Literature.

See: *Marry Me*.

RAIN PEOPLE, THE (1969)

Heart-wrenching is one way to describe the chicken scene in Francis Ford Coppola's sensitive Sixties "road picture". The story of the intertwined fates of Natalie (Shirley Knight), a pregnant Long Island housewife, "Killer" Gannon (James Caan), a simple-minded athlete and Gordon (Robert Duvall), a Nebraska motorcycle cop, paints through disappointment and unfulfilled desire a hopeful picture for all of our tomorrows.

Natalie's failed seduction of "Killer" is a resonant counterpoint to the events which follow. "Killer" finds employment as the custodian at a small roadside "zoo". Seeing the animals in their cages, he is suddenly aware of the difference between freedom and captivity. "Killer" breaks down the barriers and sets every chicken free, even the newly-hatched chicks, which he holds tenderly in his beefy hands.

It would have to be a mental "deficient", a childlike soul, who would divine the only acceptable attitude toward chickens. The chickens, young and old, are directly affected by his actions. "Killer", released from the responsibility of his job, wins his freedom — the barriers of obligation and dependence are broken down as the hens and baby chicks fly and trot away.

Neither Natalie nor Gordon understand the reason "Killer" did what he did and their relationship ends badly.

Shirley Knight and Robert Duvall survey the scene of James Caan's chicken madness.

RAMRUS, AL

Co-author of *Goin' South*. See Shaner, John Herman.

REBEL WITHOUT A CAUSE (1955)

In the history of motion pictures there are only a handful of unquestionably original chicken scenes — the chicken fantasy in Chaplin's *The Goldrush*, the chicken reality in Jack Nelson's *Chickens*,

The end of the "chicken run" in the classic 'Rebel Without A Cause'.

the chicken wedding in von Sternberg's *The Blue Angel* and the "chicken run" in Nicholas Ray's *Rebel Without a Cause*, the essential film document of mid-Century America.

"Chicken" is the one word that enrages Jim Stark (James Dean), a teenage "hot rodder" who is locked in a macho rivalry with Buzz (Corey Allen), another juvenile casualty of the New Prosperity. Before the actual chicken (or "chicky") run, Jim sits on the hood of one of the cars that he and Buzz will race across Millertown Bluff. He lights a cigarette which Buzz, in an unexpectedly intimate gesture, takes from his lips and drags on. "You know something?" Buzz says, "I like you." Jim's thoughts are elsewhere. "Why do we do this?" Buzz is too cool not to have an answer for him: "Ya gotta do something, don'tcha?"

They fire up their engines and race across the bluff. Jim's car stops at the edge. Buzz, trapped in his "hot rod", speeds over the cliff and into the sea.

Every subsequent film that deals with the subject of courage and cowardice by way of the chicken, owes a debt to Nicholas Ray's genius. He originated a concept that has since become an indispensable figure of speech in every English-speaking culture in the world.

See: *Faster Pussycat! Kill! Kill!; Joe; Rocky II; Warriors, The*.

RITCHIE, MICHAEL

A distinguished director of uniquely American films (among them, *The Candidate, Smile, Semi-Tough, Bad News Bears, Divine Madness*), Ritchie was unintimidated by anonymous warnings against communicating with us. He welcomed our overture with the words, "You are the first to realize that the (underlying) theme in my films is not competition but chickens." In his letter to us of August 13, 1980 he answers the following questions:

A. What were the contents of Bette Midler's chicken purse?

B. Is Bette Midler aware of chicken consciousness?

C. May we have a picture of you and your house?

1. Was any pressure put upon you by the studio to "lighten" the chicken scene in *Smile*?

2. What was the reaction of industry executives to that scene and its obvious implications?

3. Was the scene shot on a closed set?

4. The immediate connection between the girls of the pageant and the "exhausted rooster", which di Carlo refuses to kiss, generates tremendous sexual tension. What was the "front office" response to that?

5. Why did you choose to include such a shocking, graphic chicken scene?

6. What effect did Bruce Dern expect his part in the chicken scene to have on his career?

7. Is Michael Ritchie becoming a missionary on behalf of chicken consciousness?

8. Do you consider *Smile* to be your strongest chicken statement?

See: Landis, John; *Smile*.

MICHAEL RITCHIE

THE ISLAND

August 13, 1980

Mr. Jon-Stephen Fink
Ms. Mieke van der Linden
473 South Bedford Drive
Beverly Hills, California 90210

Dear Jon and Mieke:

Here are the answers that you requested:

Question A:

The contents of the purse are unknown except for a powder puff and cosmetic accessories.

Question B:

I have not queried Ms. Midler about chicken consciousness.

Question C:

For a picture of me and my house, consult Town & Country magazine of last June or July.

Now for the serious questions:

Question #1:

In "Smile", Nicholas Pryor played Andy DiCarlo, the reluctant chicken kisser. Since the scene was an authentic reproduction of the National Jaycee initiation ceremony, United Artists gave us the same courageous support they gave Frank Coppola in exposing the horrors of Vietnam. No other animal was considered since authenticity was foremost in my mind.

-2- August 13, 1980

Question #2:

For criticism of the above scene, please contact CBS, Department of Program Standards, which exercised severe censorship of the scene before its network airing.

Question #3:

Our closed set was penetrated by two actual Jaycees who became drunk, along with the rest of the cast, and then marvelled at our authenticity.

Question #4:

See Question 2.

Question #5:

See Question 1.

Question #6:

Contact Bruce Dern himself. For CBS censorship, he was required to use the word "chicken's end" for "chicken's ass."

Question #7:

I defer any analysis of my chicken consciousness to you and the Jaycees.

Question #8:

While "Smile" may be my strongest chicken statement, it failed to alter the national Jaycee "exhausted rooster ceremony" just as the "Candidate" failed to alter the American political scene.

I leave to future generations the task of raising or lowering chicken consciousness.

Sincerely,

Michael Ritchie

P.S. No, I will not be your pen pal but good luck on the book.

Bette Midler turning "chickenshit into chicken salad" in concert in 'Divine Madness'. Michael Ritchie, who directed, considers this scene Midler's statement, not his.

"Hanging out on Second Avenue, eating chicken vindaloo", Joey Ramone sings as the band makes its first appearance on screen. The "punks" of today hate everything except chicken.

ROCK 'N' ROLL HIGH SCHOOL (1980)

If the chicken is to remain a vital element of Western culture then each generation must find a place for it. Roger Corman has for many years provided the "youth market" with the means to find the right place for the right time.

The original American "punk" rock band, the Ramones, are director Allan Arkush's vehicle for introducing chicken consciousness to a desperate generation. The quartet burst onto the scene in a Cadillac convertible, miming their "teen anthem", "I Just Wanna Have Something To Do". These are the opening lines:

> Hanging out on Second Avenue
> Eating chicken vindaloo...

As he sings, Joey Ramone flings away the chicken leg he has been eating.

This apparent disregard both of chickens and food (except pizza) is actually a call to arms — it is the youth, on street level, who are closely in touch with chickens. The remote adult world, exemplified by Vince

Lombardi High School in general and the martinet Principal Togar in particular has forgotten the way of the chicken and exists only to stifle human spirit.

See: *A Hard Day's Night; Bad Company; Freaks; Kramer vs. Kramer.*

ROCKY II (1979)

The parallel stories of Sylvester Stallone and Rocky Balboa, the character he created, are the most convincing evidence we have of the extent of the Council's control. Whether Stallone was an accomplice or a dupe is something we can learn only from Stallone or the Council and neither has expressed a willingness to speak out on the subject.

Rocky was Sylvester Stallone's first picture deal. Incredibly, he convinced a major studio that his screenplay ought to be produced and that he should star in it. *Rocky* won an Academy Award for Best Picture. Incredible...or inevitable?

It is clear that the Council were quick to appreciate Stallone's appeal and just as quickly they formulated a plan to take advantage of it. It is difficult to account for the enormous success that *Rocky* enjoyed. In the first place, Rocky (Stallone) *loses* his fight against Apollo Creed (Carl Weathers) for the heavyweight championship. In the second place, not a single chicken appears anywhere in the film. Those two facts taken together may suggest something, but in terms of conventional film practice, it is the long way round.

The Council was looking at a bigger picture. To make full use of the folk stories of Stallone and Rocky, a new strategy needed to be developed. In Petaluma, a dozen "tourists" met and looked to the future — *Rocky II.*

In *Rocky II*, it is Apollo Creed who is spoiling for a fight with the "Italian Stallion". His problem is that Rocky doesn't want to fight again. Creed's publicist begins circulating stories that the ex-challenger is afraid to meet the Champ in a re-match. Rocky is shown a newspaper advertisement, a cartoon which pictures Creed wringing the neck of the "Italian Chicken". The war of nerves is on.

Burgess Meredith returns as Rocky's trainer, Mickey, who rouses the fighter back to action, and back into training. Speed, Mickey tells Rocky is the most important weapon in a boxer's arsenal. In his younger days, he remembers, fighters sharpened their reflexes by chasing chickens[28]. To that end, Mickey presents Rocky with a chicken to chase. Says Rocky, "I feel like a Kentucky fried idiot."

The chicken chasing scene is not gratuitous, despite the fact that it was devised by a minor Council official[29] and only directed by Stallone. Substantially it is a re-enactment of the Myth of Gilgamesh, the story of the Sumerian god-king who went in search of immortality. As an athlete, Rocky seeks that immortality by winning a championship. His successful capture of the chicken, in fact the chase itself, vividly expresses the idea that only through union with chickens can immortality (fame) be

"I feel like a Kentucky Fried idiot", Rocky complains.

Mickey's training technique teaches Rocky (Sylvester Stallone) a valuable lesson.

approached. In *Rocky II*, Rocky and chickens are intimately connected and he goes on to win the Heavyweight Championship of the world. Curiously, the film was neither nominated for nor won any Academy Award.

See: *Bad Company; Rebel Without A Cause*.

The Rogue River Rooster Crow.

ROGUE RIVER ROOSTER CROW, THE

According to the official literature, the City of Rogue River, Oregon saw its first Rooster Crow Contest in April of 1953. A trade organisation calling themselves the Rogue River Rooster Club "met to consider a proposal submitted by Shade Coombs, a fellow member...(who) had read a story about the coal miners of Wales who presented colourful rooster crowing contests during their holidays." That story of the origin of the contest has been repeated so often that it is believed to be true.

In actuality the "trade organisation" which met in the spring of 1953 was the Rogue River *Rooster* Club, all of the members of which coincidentally shared the same mailing address, "General Delivery, Kerby, Oregon." More astonishing are the identities of these "local merchants" — Rogue River was playing host to the six highest ranking members of the 1953-54 council: Edward Dmytryk, Bunny Dahl, Bud Abbott, Lee Strasberg, Dalton Trumbo and William Wyler. The purpose of their visit, far from wanting to "generate publicity and promotion for the town", was to institute a public ritual for the election of new Council presidents. The contest is the third and final Council event of the year, following the Delmarva Poultry Festival by three weeks.

The field of contestants (the roosters) are the Council's "electoral college". Each rooster is the representative of a presidential nominee. When a rooster is declared the winner, after having crowed more times than any other during 30 minutes of competition, the Council has a new president*. The form and function of motion pictures made during any given year is determined, in large measure, at the Rogue River Rooster Crow.

ROOSTER COGBURN (1975)

Writer Martin Julien spun this tale out of the rich yarn of *True Grit*. Katharine Hepburn plays Eula Goodnight the stoic, sharp-shooting evangelical forced into an exasperating relationship with the irascible Rooster Cogburn (John Wayne), an unorthodox U.S. Marshall.

The machismo of the Rooster of the title is a neat counterpoint to Hepburn's sly femininity. Rooster asserts himself sexually (romantically) and socially by scourging the frontier of demented outlaws. On a superficial level, the film's only apparent contribution to chicken consciousness is the reassurance that roosters will always crow and hens will always brood. The characters and location, however, conceal a shattering subtext.

One theme underscores every pivotal scene: the union of the sacred and the profane. Early on in their friendship, Eula helps Rooster with his writing; she calls his penmanship "chicken scrawl". At this point we know three things about Cogburn; he is big, he has one eye and he is functionally illiterate. We know one thing for certain about Eula: she is doing the Lord's work. She invokes the Bible during a harrowing scene in court, when Cogburn's commission as a lawman hangs in the balance. She compares him to Gideon and the judge answers her, "God didn't raise a Gideon here. God raised a Rooster, a wilful, strutting bird!" Cogburn wins his case and emerges from the ordeal as nothing less than the rough face of the Holy Spirit.

In the context of chicken consciousness, though, what is the "Holy Spirit"? It is the irresistible will of the Council. In the film community, *Rooster Cogburn* was regarded as crude but effective propaganda. In essence it was an explanation of the current Council policy and a justification of its methods. At that time murmurs of discontent reached

*On the first day of each quarter the Council has the option to submit the president to a vote of confidence. "Confidence" or "No Confidence" is decided on the outcome of ten successive rolls of a pair of dice, with the president rolling against each of his fellow executive board members. Unless the president "craps out", a vote of confidence is won if three of the five members roll losing numbers.

 the backrooms of Petaluma. The charges of "power mongering" had to be answered before resistance to the Council consolidated and gathered serious momentum. This film was the result of that defensive action; *power* is softened to *authority*, deriving from a holy vocation. So that the point would not be missed, the film was shot on location in the Rogue River area of Oregon, site of the annual Council presidential elections.

Rooster Cogburn was inspired by the Nazi classic, *Triumph of the Will*.

See: *Bad Company*; Rogue River Rooster Crow, The.

John Wayne strikes a suitably cocky pose as Rooster Cogburn.

ROSEMARY'S BABY (1966)

Roman Polanski, whose chickenwork is consistently original (if bizarre), invites us to consider the possibility that Evil can inhabit a human body, perverting it so that it rejects chicken.

Mia Farrow plays the innocent Rosemary Woodhouse who is cruelly used by her husband Guy (John Cassavettes) and her elderly neighbours Minnie and Roman Catevet (Ruth Gordon and Sidney Blackmore). The all too familiar story of a young girl who is raped by the Devil is given an unusual twist in this telling.

Given food to strengthen her body and that of the satanic babe growing within her, Rosemary unconsciously nibbles a plateful of chicken hearts. She sees her reflection in the toaster and instantly vomits. This is a rare instance of chicken itself being horrifying and repulsive. It is horrifying and repulsive to Evil (the evil that is, literally, inside Rosemary), and in this way Polanski portrays the chicken as the vessel of absolute Good.

If there is a unifying theme in the films of Roman Polanski, it must be the proposition that the world is remorselessly unfair. In the battle for Rosemary's heart, soul and body, Evil triumphs over the chicken.

Rosemary (Mia Farrow) reflects on a meal of raw chicken livers.

SANGER, JONATHAN

The producer of *The Elephant Man* agreed to speak with us after months of pacifying us with vague excuses ("I've got meetings all next week," and, "I know I promised to get back to you, but it's just been crazy around her," and, "Call me after the 3rd... ", etc...). Cool and aloof at first, Sanger gradually warmed to us and revealed incidents in his past which would intrigue a trained criminologist.

"I never saw a live chicken until I was 23. The first time I saw a chicken it was tied to my bed in Mexico. When I woke up in the morning, no chicken. That afternoon we ate *mole poblano*."

When we asked him to list the ingredients of *mole poblano*, he moved immediately on to the subject of the film we had met to discuss. Without responding to specific questions, he volunteered: "There are no

TWENTIETH
CENTURY-FOX
FILM CORPORATION

October 23, 1980

Mr. Jon Fink
Ms. Mieke Van der Linden
473 South Bedford Drive
Beverly Hills, CA. 90212

Dear Jon & Mieke:

These are your questions:

1. Have you been directed by the Council to deny its existence?

2. Have you been directed by the Council to deny the presence of chickens in "The Elephant Man?"

3. Will chickens never figure in any film with which you are connected?

While not wishing to appear "chicken," I forwarded your questions to my attorney in the belief that legal counsel might protect me from future reprisal (from whatever quarter.) He has assured me that a grand jury testimony based on conjecture and "to the best of my knowledge..." will be unlikely to place me in jeopardy, although I would need certain obvious indemnifications from you before answering your first question.

In responce to your second question, I have never been directed by any person or organization to deny the presence of chickens in "The Elephant Man." Nor have I been directed to affirm their presence, either. I can only admit that, to the best of my knowledge, no conscious effort was made to either include or exclude chickens from the movie. I'm sure you've heard of the pig lobby in England. "The Elephant Man," as I'm sure you will understand, was a British subsidy film qualifying for all EADY benefits. There are several "pig" scenes I could name. I trust you get my drift. We would have been extremely unwise to do anything that could have interfered with our standing as a British film. Beyond that, I must allow you to draw your own conclusions.

To your third question, I certainly wouldn't be so foolish as to state that "chickens will never be in any film with which I am connected." To eliminate, at one stroke, such a large and

TWENTIETH
CENTURY-FOX
FILM CORPORATION

Page 2

fertile basis of subject matter at this stage would be folly. In point of fact, I have held meetings with the Disney organization on a possible public domain rendering of "The Chicken Little Story." I am also working with two friends on a script that is loosely based on the life of Henny Penny. We have optioned the rights to unpublished memoirs. Zoetrope has expressed interest but I am looking for independent financing since I feel control of the material is essential in a project with a strongly instructive moral base as this one. The moral, "you get what you give" is particularly relevant to today's lethargic mass audience.

Finally, I wanted to tell you that the seminal scene to raise my chicken consciousness in film was the underrated chicken scene in "Rebel Without A Cause." It said it all.

Wings up.

Sincerely,

Jonathan Sanger

JS/led

Jonathan Sanger, producer of 'The Elephant Man'.

barnyard animals in the toys," referring to a pile of porcelain animals briefly on screen in *The Elephant Man*. Our suspicion that Sanger had been "prompted" for his meeting with us grew stronger when his conversation stiffened unnaturally, as if his "lines" had been over-rehearsed or not rehearsed enough.

"We knew about the (chicken) book. We wanted to make sure the public would think of us as an American film unlike other American films, so we kept the chickens out." We asked him point blank whether the Council had prepared his remarks or altered his personality. He spoke in a monotone, "I don't know enough about the Council"

We walked outside his office to the "New York Street" on the Fox lot, a place that reminded Sanger of his childhood. Here he seemed to feel relaxed and asked to be photographed holding a favourite object of his. He told us that he couldn't remember where or when it had come into his possession.

He became almost wistful when the shutter began to snap. "When I was at summer school at UC Berkeley in 1963 I was going out with a nursing student. Every time I had dinner at her place it was smoked chicken from her father's chicken farm in Petaluma. And hey, you know what? She always wanted to go to the movies! I can't remember her name."

When we left him, Sanger's complexion was ashen. "I have a feeling that my phone is being tapped. If I weren't aware of this previous evidence I—I don't know anymore. I used to believe in free will..."

See: Cornfeld, Stuart; *Elephant Man, The*.

SHAME (1967)

As a pair of ex-musicians caught amid a fictional civil war, Liv Ullman and Max von Sydow struggle to resist extinction. As in many films by Ingmar Bergman the symbolism is dense but not impenetrable. This consummate chicken scene is presented here in its entirety.

> They are alone and the world is coming to an end...They collect their belongings into one car, in a flurry of confused words and plans. "Where, which direction?" "Should we stay, should we hide in the woods?" "What should we do?" "Let's take the road down to the sea." "Should we take the chickens with us?" "At least they'll be something to eat." "Who's going to wring their necks?" "Not me." "Not me, either." "Shall I shoot them then?" "Have you heard of anyone shooting chickens?" "Well for God's sake, you don't expect me to cut their heads off. It gives me pain in the heart just to think about it."
>
> (Von Sydow) aims his gun and shoots. A cackle, wings beating and a rain of feathers. "I think I missed, where the hell did it go?" "Up there, on the wall." "No, I'm not going to shoot a chicken." "Leave them to live as long as they can. The eggs

 may always be of some use to someone."*

The "shame" is God's.

**Three Screenplays* by Ingmar Bergman.

See: *Annie Hall.*

Al Ramrus, John Herman Shaner, 'Goin' South' screenwriters.

SHANER, JOHN HERMAN AND AL RAMRUS

The two principal authors of *Goin' South* were candid with us about their crusade to bring chickens into popular consciousness.

"I come from a long line of chicken farmers in the Ukraine," Shaner boasted. "A lot of the lines in *Goin' South* were straight out of our mothers' mouths."

The line which came immediately to Al Ramrus was Julia's defence of boiled chicken, "Boiled is better for you." Ramrus confided, "We don't understand it ourselves."

Together, alternating sentences between them and at times, words, Shaner and Ramrus recounted their childhoods in New York. Each had worked for poulterers Storch and Gendler, whose backroom was always piled high with the kosher corpses of chickens. The job was passed from friend to friend and eventually fell to a "borderline mental defective whom we'll call 'Lester'." Lester was 14 when he went to work at Storch and Gendler. He became obsessed with inserting his penis into any hole he could find in a chicken carcass.

"We have a lot of repressed guilt about that, I guess. We have a tendency to expiate guilt through art." It was not clear whether Al meant *we*, "Al and John" or *we* in a much broader sense. We suspect he meant both.

Shaner continued. "Chicken is a Jewish animal, it's the only animal we had any intimate relationship with in New York City. I'm surprised that gentiles can relate to chickens at all."

On the subject of *Goin' South*, the writers were anxious for us to appreciate a dimension of the chicken incidents which they thought might have escaped us. Shaner explained. "Chickens are like creative movie people — they're eviscerated and devoured." He went on to make an example that proved he knew what he was talking about. "The Red Jungle Foul is a direct link to the William Morris Agency," he said in a voice barely above a whisper, "and through that company it contributes to the gene pool of Hollywood agents." Shaner let the point sink in, then said wearily, "We'd like to leave some of this behind for a while and go where the new faith is — Gitlitz's Deli in Tel Aviv. They make a *helzel** that is out of this world."

See: *Goin' South*.

SHOOTIST, THE (1976)

As an old gunman dying of cancer, John Wayne's sensitive portrayal of J.B. Books brings him closer to chickens than he had come after more than forty years of acting. Director Don Siegel chose a chicken scene of presence as great as the Duke's.

Books is taken as a boarder in the house of a widow (Lauren Bacall) and her son (Ron Howard). Books is caught in a contradiction when he has to discourage the boy, Gillom, from an interest in gunfighting at the same time he chooses for himself a "dignified" death in a gunfight with the three toughest outlaws in the territory. Gillom's disobedience to his mother is dealt with by Books in a scene which owes much to the Abraham and Isaac segment of John Huston's *The Bible*.

Gillom is waiting in the shed. Books crosses from the house. The shot is from the left and slightly above Books' shoulder. He fills the screen. As he walks across the yard we hear — but never see — chickens running for cover.

Alarmed by Books' "double standard", the hypocrisy of his "justice", the phantom clucking is a protest from the other world, from the dimension of objective truth. While the chickens attend Books' act they

* *Helzel* is a chicken neck stuffed with millet. Ground chicken oesophagus was held to be a remedy for bedwetting.

 do not endorse it, they are the "cherubs" who have no earthly power to divert him. When Books and Gillom confront each other it is Books who softens, suggesting that he perhaps "heard" the chickens in his heart.

Audiences report feeling an inexplicable sense of calm when this film is shown as the second feature of a double bill.

SIN TOWN (1929)

The world war is over and after demobilisation Silk Merrick (Hugh Allen) and Chicken O'Toole (Jack Oakie) join the Great Migration westward. Unlike scores of other veterans, they find work, hiring on as ranch hands in Arizona. Unlike scores of other ranch hands, Silk and Chicken are fired from their jobs for laziness, the first misfortune of many that will rain down on them.

Forced by poverty and hunger, they resort to chicken theft. Their plan for the chicken once they have it isn't clear — either they will hold it for ransom and so raise enough money to buy two square meals, or they will barbecue it. Neither plan has a chance to materialise. Mary Burton (Elinor Fair), whose chicken the boys are after, nabs them in the act. After that, few things go well for her.

Mary's father is murdered by Pete Laguerro (Ivan Lebedeff), the lord of Sin Town. Silk and Chicken are arrested for the crime. Silk, being altogether more agile than his partner, escapes from jail, and being altogether more foolhardy joins a band of ranchers intent on burning Sin Town to the ground. In the course of the attack on Sin Town, Silk frees Chicken from jail and captures Laguerro. Having won Mary's heart with beautiful words and brave deeds, the boys settle down with her in a comfortable *ménage à trois*.

Cecil B. DeMille made this picture with the hope that the new medium of film would carry the message of chicken morality to a great many people. His "fable" assured tham that the dark days of the Depression (Sin Town) would be ended when they accepted chickens as partners in life, as Silk and Mary (representing the masses) accepted Chicken O'Toole. Like Jack Nelson, DeMille was to be deeply disappointed. The Depression and its lingering effects remained unrelieved until the Second World War.

See: *Bad Company; It Happened One Night*.

SLEEPER (1973)

This film signalled a transitional phase in Woody Allen's work. It is the mid-point in his artistic progresssion from satire and farce to meditative comedy and drama. The chicken scene was intended to reassure his admirers that his unconventional style will never become diluted and to prepare his critics for a radical shift of emphasis.

As Miles Monroe, a 20th Century health food store owner who awakes from an ulcer operation several centuries later in a fascist America,

Allen forecasts his own future. While foraging in a forest for food, Miles discovers a "farm" where gigantic fruits and vegetables grow — a banana the size of a canoe, a strawberry that could be mistaken for a small boulder, one man-size stalk of celery and towering above them all, an awe-inspiring chicken. Miles is so moved by the sight of it they he says

Woody Allen's turn toward more serious themes was foreshadowed in the Big Chicken sequence in 'Sleeper'.

aloud, "That's a big chicken."

The "big chicken" is Allen's first experiment with the kind of poetic symbolism which characterises the work of European filmmakers such as Ingmar Bergman, Franco Brusati and Luis Bunuel. For Miles, the chicken is a manifestation of the deepest fears and greatest hopes which, in his own time, surrounded the prospect of world famine. For Allen, it is his own nightmarish image of a personal famine, a famine of the soul.

See: *Food of the Gods; Mysterious Island*.

SMILE (1975)

Michael Ritchie refers to *Smile* as his "strongest chicken statement" and with it he has brought to the screen a kind of passion play: Everyman's struggle to answer the essential question of our relationship to chickens.

135 Bob Freelander (Bruce Dern) is the chief organiser of the Young American Miss Beauty pageant sponsored by his town. He is also the *capo di tutti capi* of the Jaycees, the mystical wing of Santa Rosa's Chamber of Commerce. His friend Andy di Carlo (Nicholas Pryor) is indifferent to the pageant and all that it represents. Blind to Andy's feelings, deaf to his protests, Bob tries to press him into service and brings him to the threshold of absolute acceptance — Andy's initiation into the Jaycees.

The initiation ceremony is swathed in secrecy, set in a park at night. The initiates stand in a single file, anxious for the thing to be done, whatever that thing might be. Bob appears in front of them. He is dressed in a crude chicken costume. On a silver tray he carries a chicken carcass which is stuffed with a froth of cream. He holds the rump of the chicken to the lips of the first man in line, who humbly kisses it. And so it goes until Bob stands in front of Andy. A tense moment passes. Then, in a gesture that seems to take all of Andy's strength, he smashes the chicken to the ground and runs away into the darkness. Bob chases him, his chicken robes billowing, the limp chicken clutched in his hand.

It is this fundamentalist view that Ritchie endorses. To his mind, the time is past when we can afford the luxury of a middle ground. Either we accept the salvation that chickens offer us or we accept the fate reserved for heretics — to be pursued by the consequences of our faithlessness down all the days of our lives.

See: Ritchie, Michael.

The acceptable face of the crude chicken ritual documented by Michael Ritchie in 'Smile'.

SOME LIKE IT HOT (1959)

Billy Wilder was under tremendous pressure as a director of "hit" movies to create a chicken scene that captured the spirit of the time. The idea that animated the American public in 1959 was the belief in unlimited opportunity.

Joe (Tony Curtis) is determined to seduce Sugar (Marilyn Monroe), a woman moved by delicate sentiment and immeasurable wealth. Joe arranges to have dinner with her onboard a yacht and the dinner he serves her is a beautifully prepared chicken. While Sugar parries Joe's thrusts, Joe persistently, suggestively takes small bites out of a drumstick.

"During the shooting...Tony Curtis had to nibble forty-two chicken

'Some Like It Hot' Marilyn and Tony on the yacht.

 legs through forty-two takes because Marilyn could not get lines right. He can almost be forgiven for declaring afterwards that he would have preferred to kiss Hitler in person than Marilyn."[30]

The idea for the scene might have been suggested to Wilder by a tune that was popular at the time, "Wing Ding Daddy-o", the lyrics of which were based on an old folk song:

> The chickens are a-crowin', a-crowin', a-crowin'
> The chickens are crowin' for 'tis almost daylight.
> My mother will scold me, will scold me
> My mother will scold me for stayin' away all night.
> My father will uphold me, uphold me, uphold me
> My father will uphold me and say I done just right.[31]

See: *Exterminating Angel; Faster, Pussycat! Kill! Kill!; Private Life of Sherlock Holmes, The; Tom Jones.*

STROSZEK (1977)

Werner Herzog described this film as a ballad. It may or may not be, we leave that for others to decide. It is a poignant story of three losers who journey from Berlin to El Dorado, Wisconsin* in search of the American Dream. They find instead a frozen land of perverted ideals.

Sheitz (Clemens Sheitz), an old man with nothing more to lose, Eva (Eva Mattes), a dumb streetwalker and Stroszek (Bruno S.), a street musician, settle into a mobile home in what they believe to be the "heartland" of America. Eva gets a job as a waitress, Stroszek as a mechanic and Sheitz believes he has discovered the means to measure "animal magnetism".

Wrote Vincent Canby of the *New York Times*, "Among the dozens of images in the film I'll remember for a long time is one near the end of a chicken that can't stop dancing." The chicken's feet are in "perpetual motion" because the base of its cage is electrified. In a sense, the chicken dance is the dream that brought Sheitz, Eva and Stroszek to America, one of perpetual arrival. Of the three characters, Stroszek is most chicken-like, just as the chicken is most Stroszek-like — a creature incapable of rage or physical aggression.

No American would make a film like this.

See: *Nosferatu.*

SUNSHINE BOYS(1975)

Few writers have successfully translated esoteric theories about language, the psychology of humour or the mythopoetic function of the

*Really Railroad Flats, Wisconsin.

chicken into box office sensations*. One of the few who have is Neil Simon. His story about the reunion of two retired vaudeville comics expertly disguises profound ruminations about language, humour and chickens as the senile rambling of a forgotten entertainer.

Willie (Walter Matthau) is an old comic who tries the patience of his manager (and nephew), Ben (Richard Benjamin). Willie not only arrives late for an audition, but cannot keep in his head the name of the product he is to endorse.

BEN
Frumpies! Frumpies!

WILLIE
I still can't remember it. Because
it's not funny. I'm in this business
57 years, you learn a few things.
You know what makes an audience laugh?
Do you know which words are funny?

BEN
You told me a hundred times, Uncle Willie.
Listen, I have to get back to the office.

WILLIE
Which words are funny?

BEN
Words with a 'k' in it are funny.
I have to get back to the —

WILLIE
Words with a 'k' in it are funny.
You didn't know that, did you?
I'll tell you which words always
get a laugh.

BEN
Alka-Seltzer.

WILLIE
Alka-Seltzer is funny.

**An attempt was once made to stage a musical comedy adaptation of the life and work of Ludwig Wittgenstein entitled *Oh! Tractatus!* but financing for the production collapsed before an available theatre could be found with the capacity to support the 250 player cast and 600 voice choir.

BEN
Chicken.

WILLIE
Chicken is funny.

BEN
Pickle.

WILLIE
Pickle is funny. All with a 'k'.
'M's aren't funny. 'L's aren't funny.

BEN
Just 'k's, I know...

WILLIE
Cupcake is funny. Tomato is not
funny. Lettuce is not funny...

Of course "chicken" is "funny" for many more reasons than that it has a 'k' in it. A scientist would be able to explain the reflex in terms of neurons and synapses and negative and positive charges, but such an explanation is irrelevant to our purposes here. The laughter we feel well up from someplace deep inside us when we are at peace and chickens come to mind is the laughter of recognition, "Yes, that's me and it's my boss and it's the cop on the beat, it's all of us!" — *that* is what the laughter is.

See: Mazursky, Paul.

SUPERVIXENS (1975)

The chicken awareness in *Supervixens* is much more explicit than, for instance, the romantic poetry of *In the Realm of the Senses*, or even the primitive forcefulness of *Emmanuelle*. Russ Meyer's wit, while not more restrained, is drier than in previous films. The chicken sex scene is an intellectual rather than a sensual argument.

The earthy, Rabelaisian involvement between chickens and human beings who live their lives nearer to nature is seen by Russ Meyer as the remnant of our original innocence. Stuart Lancaster, as the husband of Supersoul (Uschi Digard), abandons her for the pleasure of a hen. His ecstasy becomes an exultation of the chickenworld, his rapture is our rapture.

Meyer's ideas about the intimate relationship enjoyed by rural chickens and the people with whom they live are substantiated in the famous Kinsey Report.

See: Lancaster, Stuart; Meyer, Russ.

SWISS MISS (1938)

In the few years just before the Second World War, film audiences saw more of the metaphysical (in a broader sense, the romantic) aspect of the chicken. Stan Laurel and Oliver Hardy* promoted this subtle apprehension with a scene that marks the end of an artistic *period* in film history.

The story is set in an Alpine village, a locale which inevitably suggests heightened sensitivity and clarity of vision. Stan has been busy plucking chickens most of the day and now he is tired and thirsty. What he would most like to drink is the brandy he knows is in the tiny keg strapped around the neck of a nearby St. Bernard. No amount of coaxing can persuade the dog to deliver his liquor to Stan.

Oliver explains to his dim-witted friend that the dog only gives brandy

*Not their real names.

 to people it rescues from death in the snow. Finally making the connection, Stan returns to the chickens. He has filled a basket with white chicken feathers and these he strews all around him. They settle into shallow drifts. Stan lies down there and starts to moan. The St. Bernard is now stirred to action and Stan gets his life-saving brandy.

The chicken, through its feathers, becomes both the illusion (snow) and the physical means of Stan's "rescue". If we were to apply contemporary critical standards to the scene it would have to be faulted for being too "preachy". No such sermon on salvation can have "a hope in hell" of conveying its message to an increasingly jaded audience. In its time though, it appealed to a public desperately in eed of reasurance that someday they would be well and happy.

TAXI DRIVER (1977)

Three-quarters of the film passes before the powder keg explodes and chickens figure in the destinies of two lonely people.

Travis (Robert de Niro) is the taxi driver in search of a purpose and Iris (Jody Foster) is the child prostitute he is compelled to rescue from a grubby pimp. They sit together eating breakfast in a seedy New York diner.

"Do you know what Matthew said to me?" Travis puts to her. "He said I could take you up to your room and do anything I wanted to...you're just his little piece of chicken."

What follows this revelation is an orgy of violence as Travis shoots his way into and out of the whorehouse that holds Iris prisoner. Iris, as a child, is naturally nearer to the chickenworld, although its presence in her life has been perverted, just as her childhood has.

Paul Schrader's screenplay, directed by Martin Scorsese, is one of the more radical responses to the modern problem of young city-dwellers growing away from chickens as they become adults. If a return to the innocence and the chicken grave of childhood can begin peacefully, neither Shrader nor Scorsese see the possibility.

See: *Kramer vs. Kramer*.

TIN DRUM, THE (1979)

"Poland is a free state..." we hear as we see a crowded marketplace, grim under the threat of rain. Sitting in the lap of an old woman, like Poland in the lap of Germany, is a large, dark hen.

In Gunter Grass' famous novel about Oscar, the little boy who decided to stop growing, death is a prominent motif. In the film by Volker Schlondorff the dead, through chickens, carry on a dialogue with the living. Ultimately, the living stop listening and the dead stop caring.

Oscar's mother, Agnès commits suicide. At her funeral, large, healthy chickens mingle with the guests. The cemetery must be the chickens' home. A Jewish toymaker (Charles Aznavour) who knew Agnès , arrives at the gravesite to honour his dead friend. He is viciously pushed away by her family and the chickens collect around his feet. Later, the old Jew poisons himself.

At the family's funeral feast the entrée is roast chicken. In the background we can see chickens move, in just the way that the graveyard chickens moved. The family is heedless to the message of the spirits of the dead, recognising no connection between the grave and their laden table.

This is a disturbing and characteristically German piece of work from start to finish.

TEWKESBURY, JOAN

"Listen, nothing could have made me happier," the writer of Robert Altman's *Nashville* said about the chicken scene she *didn't* write. "Ronee (Blakely) wrote that herself. I don't even remember mentioning chickens to her. Bob (Altman) might've, but I doubt it...I was having a little

Joan Tewkesbury, writer of 'Nashville'.

 trouble with a chicken scene I wanted to use at the end. Originally we were going to end it on a chicken farm, at a wedding, with a rooster and a hen standing in for the groom and bride. The murder at the rally was an afterthought."

Joan Tewkesbury's belief in chickens naturally led her to seek a career in film. It was only after she became close with people who were enjoying the blessings of success in the industry that she began to realise how they were alike. While most people she met shared her appreciation for chickens, few would talk about it. "It was the strangest thing. If I was talking with someone, anyone, a gaffer, a grip, a producer, just the two of us and the subject of chickens came up, all of a sudden I noticed we were whispering. If anyone else joined us, forget it — we weren't talking about chickens at all."

Since that time Tewkesbury has learned much about the nature of the currents that sweep writers, producers, directors and projects into and out of circulation. She is fortunate in that her devotion to chicken ideals is genuine and occurs naturally in her work. To her knowledge, she has never been influenced by "special interests" to give "special attention" to her chicken scenes. "The thought is a little frightening. Creative people, at least all the creative people *I* know, are involved with chickens. That's why I wasn't surprised when Ronee wrote that scene for herself...I remember a few years ago when I started hearing people at screenings say 'cluck' you know, the way Jesus freaks say 'amen', I thought it was terrific. *Finally* people are really paying attention. Look, if there are chickens in your work, that's good work and people are going to notice. But a conspiracy? A Council? Why should anything like that have to exist?"

See: *Nashville*.

TOM JONES (1963)

280 — 286 INT. THE INN AT UPTON DINING ROOM NIGHT
Tom eats a tremendous meal while Mrs. Waters watches, obviously entranced with him. As his appetite is slowly satisfied, so she gets to work on him and his eyes and attention slowly shift from the food to her.

No one who has in their memory this celebrated dinner scene can gaze upon a roast chicken unaroused. Tony Richardson accomplished three things with this period comedy: he established the model for the Sixties anti-hero, he opened a new door on chicken consciousnesss and he changed the eating habits of millions of men and women.

Albert Finney in the title role is a rake progressing from bed to bed across the English countryside. The chicken appetizer he shares with Mrs. Waters (Joyce Redman) is the sensual prelude to a sexual banquet that Richardson prudently leaves to our imagination. The foretaste is provocative. Her lips play over a fleshy drumstick, his teeth tear into the soft white meat, she glides her tongue over the exposed bone, his lips pull playfully at moist chicken skin… It's hard to imagine how sex itself can be any more exciting.

The film was not without its detractors. Critics complained that the chicken was used as a tool to aid seduction and not as a means to commune with chickens generally. In its defense, younger critics on the whole interpreted the sex between Tom and Mrs. Waters as the consummation of their relationship with the chicken. Either way, the film was embraced by a large public and for a time, chicken dinners were served without silverware, even in England.

See: *Faster, Pussycat! Kill! Kill!; Goin' South; Some Like It Hot.*

Around 7.30 a.m. on March 18 1981, the stills of the notorious roast chicken sequence from 'Tom Jones' mysteriously disappeared from our designer's office. Coincidence … or conspiracy?

2001: A SPACE ODYSSEY (1968)

The history of the Council, like the history of the world, is described, even defined, by its apologists as a constantly shifting imperfect balance between brute force and the restraint of reason. In 1968 a militant faction of the Council won control of the executive board. To be sure that the character of this new Council was clear in the minds of American film-makers, a brutal decision was made. The Council decided to "hang a nun". The director, whose integrity made him the outstanding nominee, was Stanley Kubrick.

 As is usually the case with ideologues, the "script consultants" who worked with Kubrick and Arthur C. Clarke on the screenplay of *2001* were much more concerned with displaying evidence of their authority than they were with advancing chicken consciousness. A casual, passing reference to chicken sandwiches is inserted after the Council's *primary* message is put across*.

Dr. Heywood Floyd (William Sylvester) arrives on the moon to address a meeting of fellow scientists. He is introduced as a "distinguished friend and colleague from the National Council of Astronautics." The thin disguise of the "National Council of Astronautics" quickly falls away and then we are suddenly, unmistakably confronted by the reality of the Chicken Council; Floyd is the embodiment of the new regime.

FLOYD

> Hello everybody. Nice to be back again. Well, first of all, I bring a personal message from Dr. Howell who has asked me to convey his deepest appreciation for the many sacrifices you have had to make. And, or course, his congratulations on your discovery, which may prove to be *among the most significant in the history of science.*
>
> Now, I know there have been some conflicting views held by some of you regarding the need for complete security in this matter. More specifically, your opposition to the *cover story* created to give the impression that there is an epidemic at the base. I understand that beyond it being a matter of principle many of you are troubled by the concern and anxiety this story of an epidemic might cause your friends and relatives on earth. Well, I, uh, completely sympathize with your negative views. I find this cover story personally embarrassing myself. However, I accept the need for *absolute security* in this and I hope you will, too.
>
> Now, I'm sure you are all aware of the *extremely grave potential for cultural shock and social disorientation* contained in this present situation *if the facts were prematurely and suddenly made public* without adequate preparation and conditioning. Anyway, *this is the view of the Council ...***

Graciously, Floyd asks his audience if there are any questions. There is only one: "How much longer will this cover story have to be maintained?"

**The actual chicken scene takes place in a "moonbus" transporting Dr. Floyd and others to the site of the uncovered monolith. Dr. Halvorsen (who introduced Floyd at the earlier meeting) and Michaels (who asked Floyd the question concerning the cover story) hold a lunchbox between them. Michaels*: "Anybody hungry?" *Floyd*: "What's this? Chicken?" *Michaels*: "Something like that. Tastes the same, anyway."

**Author's italics

FLOYD

...I suppose it will be maintained as long as it is deemed necessary by the Council ... Oh, yes, um ... as some of you already know, the Council has requested that formal security oaths are to be obtained in writing from anyone who has any knowledge of this event.

The iron grip of this fanatical administration was finally broken in 1971 when it failed to win a vote of confidence. Its members were purged and now hold junior executive positions in various advertising agencies.

WARRIORS, THE (1979)

Forthwith they flye Chickens,
The way they stopt Eagles.

— William Shakespeare

Walter Hill formulated a chicken scene in the classic mode of teenage subculture films. Tuned in to adolescent anxiety, the story revolves around persistent threats to the safety of a teen "gang", danger which has to be answered with acts of physical courage.

Based on a successful play written many years ago in Persia, Hill's Warriors are a Coney Island street gang slanderously accused of murdering a criminal messiah. Pursued across every borough in the city of New York, their first confrontation is with a ragged inner-city gang called the Orphans.

The Orphans are prepared to allow the Warriors safe passage across their "turf", in the words of their leader, "There's nothin' wrong with you makin' it through our territory as long as you come in peace." At that moment, offscreen, we hear a chorus of derisive clucking from the mouth of the Orphans' "old lady", Mercy (Deborah van Valkenberg). She calls her "home boys" chicken and so causes a street fight that leaves a score of Orphan casualties and leads her into a liaison with Swan (Michael Beck), the Warriors' chief.

The success that *Warriors* enjoyed in Europe is regarded in Petaluma as a consequence of this scene. Teenagers the world over relate to the experience which brings together sexuality, violence, chickens and physical survival, even though Mercy's breasts are never clearly shown.

See: *Rebel Without a Cause*.

Lew Weitzman (The Agent).

WEITZMAN, LEW

Agent: 1. a person or thing that performs actions or is able to do so. 2. an active force or substance producing an effect... 3. a person, firm, etc., empowered to act for another.[32]

These thirty words from one succinct answer to two questions often asked before and after film contracts are signed — *What is an agent?* and *What does an agent do?* The dictionary definition is useful only if we see it to be the shadow of the truth. The truth must be discovered through direct experience.

Before we sought him out we were advised that Lew Weitzman "puts more packages together than the U.S. Post Office". We expected that if he were willing to speak, hitherto undisclosed facts about the connections between movie deals and chickens would come to light. We were not disappointed.

"This town is haunted by the fear of the unknown. It's better for me to talk than to keep quiet, believe me. I think there's an attitude among certain elements, I don't want to name names, but people in powerful positions *feather their nests* through the labour of others. I'm sure you understand what I mean." We nodded and said nothing. Weitzman went on without our needing to ask another question. As he spoke an invisible burden seemed to fall away. He asked his secretary to hold all of his calls until after our meeting was over.

"Look, you come to me with a script. You say to me, 'Lew, can you move this for me?' and I have to ask you, what's the chicken count. It's arithmetic. The more chickens the better my chances are of getting action on the production end. Usually." Clearly there was more to the deal-making process than simple arithmetic. "There's an ebb and flow of demand, not for chickens *per se*, but for certain kinds of chicken scenes. It depends on all kinds of things — the time of year, what was in the market last year, who's in, who's out — many, many variables. That's the real job of an agent, to know who is looking for what kind of chicken work when."

Weitzman then used a piece of industry slang we had not heard before. "As a matter of fact, I have to be downtown at one fifteen to stroke the beak." We nodded and said nothing. Then he explained about Chicken Boy.

See: Chicken Boy.

WHAT'S UP, TIGER LILY? (1967)

Woody Allen was not directly responsible for the chicken occurence in this film. He is responsible for leaving it uncut from his reworking of the original Japanese footage. Dubbing American voices over foreign films and thus altering the original is not an unusual practice. It was done with many famous films including, *Easy Rider* (a Czechoslovakian travelogue), *Black Like Me* (an Italian comedy) and *Psycho* (a French Health Ministry film on personal hygiene). The Japanese spy movie that was the source for *What's Up, Tiger Lily?* featured a villain whose pet and favourite murder weapon was a cobra. At feeding time the snake's entrée is a live rooster.

The sexual symbolism is obvious, and in terms of the later development of Allen's work, much more primary. The theme though, is one which would become more sophisticated through *Manhattan* and *Stardust Memories*. Two potent phallic symbols, the snake and the cock, fight for supremacy. The lower sexual urge (the snake) must kill and consume the higher romantic spirit in order to survive. In the end the picture that Allen chooses to show us is despairing, the earthly overcomes the ethereal, Ariel is destroyed by Caliban.

See: *Cockfighter*.

WIZARD OF OZ, THE (1939)

There had been two early attempts to bring Frank L. Baum's magical book to the screen, one in 1910 and another in 1924. Victor Fleming had seen them both and he was heartily disappointed that neither film made any serious attempt to portray chickens in any way that approached their true dimension. His affection for the story combined with his devotion to chickenkind and the result was a film that has established itself as an American tradition.

The early scenes, showing Dorothy (Judy Garland) on her aunt's and uncle's Kansas farm, are virtual sonnets on the intimacy that rural society enjoys with chickens. Wherever there are people who share some closeness with Dorothy, there are chickens who share that same closeness with those people.

When she and her house and her little dog are swept away on the winds of a tornado, and come to rest in Munchkinland, every detail of Dorothy's life becomes transformed. The friendly farm hands become a Scarecrow, a Tin Woodsman and a Cowardly Lion; a mean-tempered neighbour becomes the Wicked Witch of the West; a travelling patent-medicine salesman becomes a Wizard; the chickens become Munchkins. Munchkinland is humanity's ultimate destination, the heaven of chickens, the place (actually the *state*) where human and chicken merge into a single form.

Dorothy's companions, the Scarecrow (Ray Bolger), the Tin Man (Jack Haley), the Cowardly Lion (Bert Lahr) and the Wizard (Frank Morgan) are each faces of the human character — ignorance and intelligence, insensitivity and compassion, weakness and strength, charlatanism and spirituality — and the "munchickens" attend them all. Fleming holds an enchanted-looking glass up to the world and the world's reflection is the Emerald City.

The president of the Council during the last quarter of the 1937-38 session was Mervyn LeRoy, who also seized the opportunity to produce *The Wizard of Oz*. Together with Fleming and designer Cedric Gibbons, LeRoy fashioned a work that stands as a cathedral to chicken consciousness. He foresaw a time when the public at large would respond *en masse* to the timeless message of such a motion picture. As it happened, his time as chickenkind's standard bearer was drawing to a close. He was replaced as Council president in December of 1939. His successor was Huntz Hall.

NOTES

1. Petaluma, California. Population 32,000; Altitude 17′. The city once celebrated as The Egg Basket of the World is located 70 miles north of San Fancisco on Interstate 101. Demand for Petaluma's eggs and chickens reached an early peak during World War I when the poultry community shipped 450,000,000 eggs across the country and around the world. After a brief post-war slump Petaluma again became a chicken boom town. The years of prosperity continued through the early 1950's. It was around this time that the Council began to meet formally, at first in bars, in Petaluma. Here well known producers, directors, writers and agents could merge into the faceless crowd to conduct their business in perfect secrecy. Despite its decline (perhaps because of it) Petaluma remains the ultimate symbol of chicken consciousness. Council members traditionally, and no doubt genuinely, regard Petaluma with a reverence usually associated with places like Mecca, Jerusalem, Lourdes and Angkor Wat .

2. Smith, Page and Charles Daniel, *The Chicken Book*, Little, Brown and Company Boston, 1975. See Part One, Chapter 8, page 155. This book is the single most important modern document of the destiny shared by chickens and human beings.

3. Kemp, Vernon, *Journals of the Ninth Beatle*, published privately in Liverpool in 1970.

4. "The Reverend Edmund Saul Dixon, rector of Intwood-with-Keswick, wrote in the introduction of his *Treatise on the History and Management of Ornamental Poultry*, published in London in 1849, 'Poultry (is)...a class of creatures inferior to few on the face of the earth in beauty...are disregarded and disdained.' " Dixon believed strongly in the idea that chickens appeared on earth "produced by a Creative Power." (From, *The Chicken Book*.)

5. Blount, Auguste (ed.), *Comedic Stage Dialogues*, Lyttle and Sons, New York, 1921.

6. "The fighting cock was also a symbol for the ancients of unwillingness to lead a servile life..." (*The Chicken Book*. See Part One, Chapter 5, pages 73-74.)

7. von Sternberg, Josef, *The Blue Angel, An Authorised Translation of the German Continuity*, Simon & Schuster, New York, 1968.

8. Ibid.

9. Landis, John, *Universal Memories*, Unpublished.

10. Dexter, Hugo, Address to the Second Annual Convention of the American Foundation for the Advancement of Chicken Consciousness. Copyright AFACC 1976.

11. Lustig, H.L. and Nathan Windsor, *The Id, The Ego and the American Conscience — The Wars of Chicago 1920 — 1935,* Tilamook Press (Chicago) 1956.

12. Transcript of the March 27, 1954, session of the House Un-American Activities Committee,Vol. XXII, page 289.

13. Taken from *Webster's New World Dictionary of the American Language*, World Publishing Company, New York, 1957.

14. Biggs, Noel, *Movies For Everyone*, Apeline Press, St. Louis, 1968.

15. *The Chicken Book*, See Part Two, Chapter One, page 163.

16. Ibid.

17. Ibid.

18. Ibid.

19. From a conversation with Lamarr Whitney Young, Council Executive Board Member during the 1972-73 session. Our interview took place in a room at the Hollywood Hawaiian Motel, at Mr. Young's request on September 1, 1980.

20. Jordan, Rene, *Gable*, Pyramid Books, New York, 1973.

21. Ibid.

22. From a conversation with Bunny Dahl at his home, shortly before his death in 1978.

23. Dr. Dexter coined this phrase on the morning after the evening that he finished reading *The Seven Pillars of Wisdom*, by T.E. Lawrence.

24. Transcript of a tape recording of an executive session of the Council in Petaluma, which took place on January 2, 1978.

25. Xian Wen Wang, speaking at the reception for a meeting of ornamental poultry fanciers in Long Beach, California on March 18, 1979. The remark was read into the minutes of a branch meeting of the AFACC on March 19, 1979.

155 26. *The Chicken Book*, (See Part One, Chapter Two, page 38).

27. O'Bannon, Dan, excerpt from *A Live Chicken*, copyright Dan O'Bannon 1978.

28. "Although chickens have lived in the closest proximity with man for thousands of years, often, in peasant communities, sharing the same quarters, they have an understandable wariness about their human neighbours. They are proverbially hard to catch. Men...have been chasing chickens since they were first domesticated with, on the whole, indifferent success. The particular chicken...seems to know instantly that it has been singled out for special attention...If pursued, it darts and dashes with the skill and unpredictability of a broken-field runner..." *The Chicken Book*, Part Two, Chapter 15, pages 331-32.

29. From a conversation with John Landis which took place in his office at Universal Studios on October 9, 1980. This fact is alluded to in his letter of the same date.

30. Sinclair, Marianne, *Those Who Die Young*, Plexus, London, 1978.

31. *The Chicken Book*, See Part One, Chapter 8, page 155.

32. Taken from *Webster's New World Dictionary of the American Language*, (see above).

LIST OF TITLES

157 A BRIDGE TOO FAR
A HARD DAY'S NIGHT
ALL THAT JAZZ
ALL THE PRESIDENT'S MEN
ALICE DOESN'T LIVE HERE ANYMORE
ANIMAL HOUSE
ANNIE HALL
APOCALYPSE NOW
BABE RUTH STORY, THE
BAD COMPANY
BADLANDS
BEING THERE
BLUE ANGEL, THE
BLUES BROTHERS, THE
BONNIE AND CLYDE
BREAD AND CHOCOLATE
BRIDE OF FRANKENSTEIN, THE
BUGSY MALONE
BUTTONS
CATCH-22
CHICKENS
CHICKEN EVERY SUNDAY
CHINATOWN
CITIZEN CANE
CLOSE ENCOUNTERS OF THE THIRD KIND
COCKFIGHTER
COCONUTS
COMEDIANS, THE
CUL-DE-SAC
DAYS OF HEAVEN
DAY OF THE LOCUST
DARK STAR
DISCREET CHARM OF THE BOURGEOISIE, THE
DOCTOR DOLITTLE
EGG AND I, THE
ELEPHANT MAN, THE
EMMANUELLE
ERASERHEAD
EXTERMINATING ANGEL
FANTÔME DE LA LIBERTÉ, LE
FASTER, PUSSYCAT! KILL! KILL!
FIVE EASY PIECES
FOOD OF THE GODS
FOX, THE
FREAKS
FRENCH CONNECTION II
GHOST AND MR. CHICKEN, THE
GODFATHER, PART II, THE

GOIN' SOUTH
GOLDRUSH, THE
GONE WITH THE WIND
HIS GIRL FRIDAY
HISTORY OF THE WORLD, PART I
IN THE REALM OF THE SENSES
IT HAPPENED ONE NIGHT
JOE
KING KONG
KRAMER VS. KRAMER
LA DOLCE VITA
LACOMBE, LUCIEN
LAWRENCE OF ARABIA
LONGEST YARD, THE
MA AND PA KETTLE AT HOME
MARRY ME
MIDNIGHT EXPRESS
MYSTERIOUS ISLAND
NASHVILLE
NETWORK
NEXT STOP, GREENWICH VILLAGE
NIGHTMARE ALLEY
NOSFERATU
PAT GARRETT AND BILLY THE KID
PATTON
PLUCKED
PRIVATE LIFE OF KING HENRY VIII, THE
PRIVATE LIFE OF SHERLOCK HOLMES, THE
PROFESSOR, BEWARE
PROPHECY
RAINMAKER, THE
RAIN PEOPLE, THE
REBEL WITHOUT A CAUSE
ROCK 'N' ROLL HIGH SCHOOL
ROCKY II
ROOSTER COGBURN
ROSEMARY'S BABY
SHAME
SHOOTIST
SIN TOWN
SLEEPER
SMILE
SOME LIKE IT HOT
STROSZEK
SUNSHINE BOYS, THE
SUPERVIXENS
SWISS MISS
TAXI DRIVER

TIN DRUM, THE
TOM JONES
2001: A SPACE ODYSSEY
WARRIORS, THE
WHAT'S UP, TIGER LILY
WIZARD OF OZ, THE

FOR FURTHER VIEWING

ADVENTURE OF SHERLOCK HOLMES' SMARTER BROTHER, THE
ALIEN
BARABBAS
BARRY LYNDON
BATTLE OF THE BULGE, THE
BLACK STALLION, THE
BREAKING AWAY
BRINKS JOB, THE
CAPTAIN NEWMAN, MD.
CHICKEN CHRONICLES, THE
CHICKENS COME HOME
COAL MINER'S DAUGHTER
COOL HAND LUKE
COTTONPICKIN' CHICKENPICKERS
DEATH WISH
DIVINE MADNESS
DUELLISTS, THE
EASY RIDER
EMMANNUELLE IN BANGKOK
END OF THE ROAD, THE
EVEN DWARFS STARTED SMALL
FAMILY PLOT
FIDDLER ON THE ROOF
FORBIDDEN ZONE, THE
FORTUNE, THE
FREEBIE AND THE BEAN
FRENZY
GREAT SANTINI, THE
HAROLD AND MAUD
HIRED HAND, THE
HOW THE WEST WAS WON
IDOLMAKER, THE
IGORATA, THE LEGEND OF THE TREE OF LIFE
IN GOD WE TRUST
JASON AND THE ARGONAUTS
KID BLUE
LAST VALLEY, THE

LET'S SCARE JESSICA TO DEATH
LOVE AT FIRST BITE
MELVIN AND HOWARD
MISFITS, THE
MRS. WIGGS OF THE CABBAGE PATCH
MUPPET MOVIE, THE
MY MAN GODFREY
NEVER GIVE A SUCKER AN EVEN BREAK
NEW CENTURIANS
NIGHTMOVES
NORWOOD
OF MICE AND MEN
OKLAHOMA!
OUTLAW, THE
PAINT YOUR WAGON
PASSENGER, THE
PINK FLAMINGOES
QUADROPHENIA
QUIET DAYS IN CLICHY
REAL LIFE
ROSE, THE
SATURDAY NIGHT FEVER
SECRET LIFE OF AN AMERICAN HOUSEWIFE, THE
SERGEANT YORK
SONS OF KATY ELDER
STAGECOACH
STARDUST MEMORIES
START THE REVOLUTION WITHOUT ME
STUNTMAN, THE
TESS
TEXAS CHAINSAW MASSACRE, THE
THIRD MAN, THE
TOM HORN
TO CATCH A THIEF
TO FORGET VENICE
TREE OF THE WOODEN CLOGS, THE
TRIBUTE
TRUE GRIT
TWINKLE, TWINKLE, "KILLER" KANE
VILLAGE OF THE GIANTS
WHEN TIME RAN OUT
WISE BLOOD
WITH SIX YOU GET EGGROLL

ACKNOWLEDGEMENTS

When we signed the contract which commissioned us to produce this work (and warranted Virgin Books to publish it) we understood that from that moment our personal safety could not be guaranteed. As a defence against possible "interference", our friends made certain "safe houses" available to us. In order to protect these people from any kind of reprisal for providing us with sanctuary and, at the same time, to thank them publicly for their kindness and concern, our consciences allowed us no choice but to express our appreciation here. These are *not* their real names.

Cathy Meeus and Martyn Harris, our thanks for warming the month of November.

Steve Barron, our thanks for shelter of all kinds in the winter and spring.

Judy Gortikov, our thanks for sustaining us, body and soul, all summer long.

In addition, we would like to thank the members of the film community who unselfishly participated in this work. These people are Bob Anderson, Steve Barron (the real one), "Robert Benton", Mel Brooks, Ellen Burstyn, Stuart Cornfeld, Monte Hellman, Buck Henry, Stuart Lancaster, John Landis, Paul Mazursky, Russ Meyer, Dan O'Bannon, Alan Parker, Al Ramrus, Michael Ritchie, Jonathan Sanger, John Herman Shaner, Joan Tewkesbury and Lew Weitzman.

May your houses increase.

Jon-Stephen Fink *Mieke van der Linden*

Photographs Courtesy of:

Mieke van der Linden	Frontispiece, pp.25, 28, 38, 45, 53, 78, 82, 87, 90, 95, 96, 105, 112, 129, 131, 142, 147, 163.
MGM	pp.9, 41, 67, 75, 140.
Acmé Newspictures	p.12
United Press International	p.12
US Dept. of Agriculture	p.13
Joseph E. Levine	p.17
National Film Archives	pp.18, 36, 43, 50, 65, 71, 74, 85, 136.
Universal	pp.20, 38, 59, 70, 92, 127.
Allied Artists	p.26
Paramount	pp.27, 32, 72, 100, 128.
Warner Bros.	pp.33, 40, 66, 118, 119, 121.
Alan Parker Films	pp.40, 97, 106.
20th Century Fox	pp.46, 58, 69, 104.
Long Road Productions	p.47
American International	p.65
Irving Lippman	p.80
Columbia	p.98
Sheedy and Long	p.102
Pathé News	pp.108, 109.
United Artists	pp.115, 124, 135.
New World Pictures	p.122.